AMERZONIA

MARK WALTERS

Prices mentioned throughout this book have been converted from the local currency into British Pounds (£) using the exchange rates in the respective countries at the time I was in them. (£1 = €1.1 = $1.3)

LOS ANGELES TO TIJUANA

For two traits my personality is below "normal": slightly for "appreciativeness", a lot for "nervousness". He hones in on the nervousness. It requires, he tells me, urgent attention. He asks if I agree.

I tell him I don't.

Not his opinion, he says; he can only analyse the results.

He speaks like he's a doctor and I'm his patient. That's also how this cubicle we're in is set up: him at a desk on a leather swivel chair; me on a small basic chair — a chair that's set at a weird angle to him, locked in position. He's not a doctor, though, nor even a professional. He's a "volunteer". They're all "volunteers". And they're all dressed the same: black-and-white sharply-tailored uniforms.

He tells me that my foot is tapping, that I'm chewing gum.

Well, yes, I think, I'm nervous at *this* moment. But these are strange circumstances. He's a Scientologist. This is a

Scientology centre. A few minutes ago I was plugged into a sci-fi-looking "e-meter".

Maybe I shouldn't have come; I should have walked right by, gone to throw eggs at Mariah Carey as she imprints her hands and feet into the forecourt of Grauman's Chinese Theatre.

So what happened?

I was strolling Hollywood Boulevard, and there in the street outside a glass-fronted, brightly-lit building — that could pass as a bank — were these young things, smart and slick, a few sexy, flyering:

Oxford Capacity Analysis
Free Personality Test
Limited Time

In just one hour you can test the 10 key personality traits that determine your future success and happiness, and find out how to improve them. Give yourself the knowledge of you.

I twigged they were Scientologists. I was suspicious.

The woman said not to believe what the press says, that to know the truth you must go to the source.

I thought: You can't always believe the source: I'll tell you my books are great; reviews on Amazon say otherwise.

I said to her, "You'll fake my results, make them look bad in some way, and tell me you can help me if I sign up."

She said, "No, we won't; really, we won't," and holding out her little finger for me to wrap with mine, "Pinky promise."

I wrapped my little finger with hers: Is that legally binding? I doubt it. But, Why not?, I thought; Scientology is a religion — of sorts — and I've been to temples and mosques, spoken with priests and monks. And this is Los Angeles, the cradle of Scientology: The first Church of Scientology opened in LA, and the city has the largest concentration of Scientologists in the world.

So in I came to do the test, which, it transpired, was three tests. For an hour and a half I sat in a bright white room at the back of the building, answering questions with a pencil.

The Oxford Capacity Analysis was 200 questions, which I had to mark as agree, disagree, or maybe. Questions ranged from tame: "Do you often sing or whistle?"; to deep: "Is your life a constant struggle for survival?"; to odd: "Do you get occasional twitches of your muscles when there is no logical explanation for it?"

The IQ test — to be precise, the Novis Mental Ability Test — was hard. 80 questions in 30 minutes, multiple choice. I did well, scored 126, despite them trying to trip me up: On the answer sheet were 4 columns, 20 A–D rows in each column; 1 wasn't at the top left — as it should be — but in the top right, and 80 in the bottom left. Anyone not noting that — I didn't until five minutes in and had to rub out and re-enter my answers — would have flunked.

The other test, a dozen questions, was a piece of piss. At least I thought it was. But, he tells me now, I didn't do well, that I took 3 minutes when the average is 90 seconds, and that I find it hard to follow simple instructions. I can't believe I did badly on that test. A middle-schooler would have aced it.

"Let me see my paper," I say. "Show me what I got wrong."

He won't let me see it.

But my nervousness — which I haven't yet agreed with him about — is his favoured subject. He tells me my nervousness is holding back my happiness, which is only in the normal range.

I say I'm happy my happiness is in the normal range. I don't want to be a rah-rah sunshine cheerleader. Besides, I'm British, and most Brits are genetically miserable; that I'm even in the normal range of happiness is welcome.

I ask, "What would you rate your happiness as on the chart?"

He refuses to answer, says we're here to talk about me not him.

The conversation becomes awkward. Extended pauses; overly long eye contact. *Why is that?* he likes to ask. And, *Can you explain?* Always trying to elicit more; fishing, probing my past, angling for something unpleasant, searching for a crack to sledgehammer. Someone at a low ebb, short on assertiveness, would be steamrollered. But I know his game, these tactics.

We verbal fence for half an hour until he realises I'm not the droid he's looking for. I leave with a brochure — that details a range of courses and books and DVDs — and a feeling of unease: I'm in their database, name and results logged, interview probably recorded.

It wasn't, though, a waste of time: I have a certificate to prove that I'm 80% normal. I'll add that to my CV.

Back on Hollywood Boulevard — nervously checking over my shoulder, paranoid that I'm being tailed — I walk under lanky palms along the star-studded sidewalk, passing eclectic eye-candy: Classical and Chinese, Art Deco and Egyptian. I see Capitol Records, that's built like a stack of LPs, from where spun the likes of Frank Sinatra and The Beach Boys. I see the birthplace of the Oscars: the Roosevelt Hotel; and rigging for Paramount: lights shine, people scurry — hundreds of thousands of dollars for a snippet of silver screen. Everywhere are snap-happy tourists hungry for a slice of the dream, to see it, smell it, touch it. They gaze at the names immortalised in the five-point stars — Tarantino, DeVito, Foxx — with respect and reverence, as if the person is buried there. They pay to spell out their name on blank stars, and to pose for photos with Spiderman and Shrek, and they insert $10 into metal boxes for movie star maps — "Find out where the stars live! Updated every 90 days." A kitschy charade: but what else could it be? It's a stand-in for the La-La Land image of LA, which is a myth; and if it ever existed — the fifties, maybe — it's long gone, stars and studios scattered across the city, the state, the country. It's in fact more grit than glitz. Hustlers and hawkers accost, alcoholics stagger and slur. Homeless are splayed limply across the stars; tourists step over them. "Give me some change? Man, a quarter?" says a glassy-eyed panhandler draped in a duvet, slumped against the window of one of the many tattoo parlours. Neon signs blink on seedy stores that sell bongs, trashy lingerie, crappy trinkets. In windows and on trashcans are posters for strip joints, for tarot readings. Placards advertise sales — "Everything's $5" — or quotes from the Bible. A Jesus fan-club chant that gays are going to hell; a speeding LAPD car, red lights flashing, siren wailing — a mugging, probably, or an altercation;

crimes too bland for the cinema. And above, in the background, crowning the rocked, tawny hills of Mount Lee, the most famous sign in the world. Nine white letters that are an analogy, perhaps, for what they represent: when I walk up for a look, a loudspeaker yells at me: "This is a restricted area; leave immediately."

Hollywood is fantasy, as pretend as the movies produced, but the so-called Platinum Triangle of Holmby Hills, Beverly Hills, and Bel Air — a bus ride along Sunset Boulevard from Hollywood — is closer in spirit and style to the mythical Tinseltown; is sugar-coated, stardust-sprinkled. I've come on a tour. Better in a group than alone, I reason; a man on himself is a stalker. But being in a group, I feel like a tit. Discreet we're not. Louis, the guide, has a hairdo that looks like a pineapple and carries a boombox on his shoulder that blasts tunes about LA. We walk in single file like school children visiting a zoo. Other groups are in open-top buses; some have brought binoculars, as if they're on a twisted safari: *And there, in the bushes, is the rarely-seen Clooney.*

I ask Louis if he ever sees stars on his tour.

Yes, he says, but rarely.

Not that I care if I see one. To meet a star in person can only be a letdown. They won't be as cool or sexy as they are on screen. They'll be fatter or duller or sadder — or all three. And what is there to say? "Thanks for pretending to save the world."

We turn off Sunset Boulevard and walk along Ladera Drive to Monovale Drive. This is Holmby Hills: Not as famous as its neighbours, says Louis, but more exclusive, more expensive. Rhianna, Rourke, Affleck, and Ellen are some of the current residents — at least they own properties in Holmby Hills; they also own properties elsewhere, so aren't often here.

"Who else?" I ask. "It can't all be stars."

Puppet masters that pull the strings, Louis says, and entrepreneurs and CEOs. Google gazillionaire Eric Schmidt, for example.

The streets are spic and span but without a sidewalk — because no one who lives in Holmby Hills walks anywhere. So we walk in the gutter like the scum that we are. We pass faux-French chateaus and Tudor-style residences, preposterous properties that verge on palaces — to call them houses is to grossly understate. Dollar-green hedges thick as the walls of vaults make it difficult to catch more than glimpses. As well as strategic foliage, Heaven-like gates guarded by porky Peters.

Louis talks as we walk: ". . . Elvis Presley lived there . . . That one was Frank Sinatra . . . This was where Mick Jagger lived . . . Walt Disney was up there . . . Jacko died here . . ."

Jackson's promotor rented the house for him at a cost of $100,000 per month. It recently sold for $18 million.

Most in Holmby Hills are priced above $10 million; many are nearer to $100 million. Carolwood Drive, where we walk next, is one of the most expensive streets on earth. Astronomical price tags but they get a lot for their money: double-digit bedrooms, wine cellars and cinemas, bowling lanes and libraries, salons and gyms and spas.

Beyond my budget, even if I become Bryson 2.0. But then an opportunity presents itself: A sign on a lamppost: Lost; reward offered; a picture of a three-legged dog named Peanut. The reward could be the GDP of Fiji. And how hard can it be to find? With a leg missing, it's probably running in a circle. If I can't locate Peanut, I could kidnap another. A dog, maybe a child — the higher the risk, the higher the reward. I wouldn't harm them, just take them to the cinema for a few hours. If the parent hadn't paid $10 million by then, I'd give the kid back for the price of the cinema tickets.

Next we cross Sunset Boulevard to Charing Cross Road, where is the most expensive house ever to sell in Los Angeles, $100 million in 2016: The Playboy Mansion. Tied to its gate are bunnies and panties, in honour to Hefner who died a month ago. Then down South Mapleton Drive, past more hedges and more gaudy mega-mansions, more Lamborghinis and Hummers and Bentleys, to the Big Momma of Holmby Hills, indeed of Los Angeles: The Manor, owned by Petra Ecclestone, daughter of Formula One tycoon Bernie. The largest house in Los Angeles, she paid — or, I suspect, her father paid — $85 million for it six years ago. It's for sale now for $200 million. Though it's larger than the White House, and more luxurious than Wills or Harry will ever live in, I'm not awed. I think: Inside those walls you're the same as us: your days spent sitting on the sofa, staring at screens. Your toilet might be gold-plated, but your shit still stinks.

I take the subway to downtown. From there a walk to the Greyhound station. A walk through Skid Row. I'd been warned not to walk here, but I thought it can't be that bad. But it is that bad. A blackhole of homelessness, even in daylight it looks as if night. Septic streets of chain-link fences and graffitied shutters, of scattered garbage and strewn liquor bottles, of human faeces and streams of urine, of needles in gutters, dead rats, decay. Rows of tents, ripped and stained, for block after bleak block; also dens and tarps and lean-tos, soiled mattresses and filthy threadbare furniture. Some are curled up on flattened cardboard boxes beneath boarded-up windows. Some are wrapped head-to-toe in blankets, looking like body bags, corpses set for the morgue.

Not tens, or even hundreds; thousands, thickening the air with their smell, the stench of unwashedness, of unwantedness. So many they spill off the sidewalk into the roads of Skid Row. They sleep or sit, or limp, skulk, forage, wander with seeming aimlessness. They push carts and prams, trundle broken-wheeled shopping trolleys. Some wait in line for a meal, for toilet paper or shampoo. The queues outside charities and missions, the homeless services concentrated in this neglected district. The 1970s policy of "containment" located these services in this area, in turn creating a teeming dystopia in downtown Los Angeles for the discarded destitute to congregate and fester. For the homeless, Skid Row became "home".

No age spared, no ethnicity. Plenty sport scars and scabs and sores. Some are lame, blind, palsied. Many are visibly disturbed. A woman is half-naked (the lower half). Others scream or cry curses — aimed sometimes at one another, sometimes at themselves. One on a corner, seemingly high on something, looks to be doing a stand-up comedy routine in which he's both the comedian and the audience. Another argues with himself and appears to be losing the argument.

It's as if there's been a mass breakout from the asylum. Not just here; all over LA. On Hollywood Boulevard there was a commotion then a chase; someone called after the chaser: "Hey, does that guy have a gun?"

Still in chase, he said back: "Nah, man; he was masturbating."

The homeless, the crazies: as much a part of the Los Angeles streetscape as the palm trees, the convertibles, the knock-off superheroes. In streets and parks, on subway trains and platforms, living like trolls under bridges and freeway ramps. It has more unsheltered people than any US city. In New York, shelter is by law provided; only a small proportion putrefy on the street. Whereas three-quarters of LA's homeless are unsheltered. A recent count recorded 55,000 homeless in the county — up more than 25% from last year.

The vibe is gnarly, and I'm a beacon. The stares speak, but there are words too. "What dat sonovabitch doin' here?" I hear a man say as I pass.

Someone else calls me "skinny jeans" and yells an insult I don't quite catch.

Another shouts, "Faggot."

After several blocks I skip walking and jump on a local bus for the final stretch to the station.

The bus from Los Angeles to San Diego takes three hours, and the train from San Diego to San Ysidro forty-five minutes. There: a high wall, barbed wire, spotlights, cameras, patrol cars, guards. It passes as a prison, but it's not. A head-height metallic turnstile; above in bold, block letters: MEXICO.

The eyesore stretches beyond sight. I've seen nothing as fortress-like at any other border. This is what Trump wants for the 3000-kilometre length of the US-Mexico border. At a cost of ten-plus billion dollars. A cheaper, prettier option would be a hedge. But Trump wouldn't be president had he said, "I will grow a great, great hedge on our southern border, and Mexico will pay for the seeds."

The irony: not so long ago — the mid-1800s — California was in Mexico. The US started a war against their southern neighbours, and as part of the peace negotiations Mexico ceded California — also Nevada, Arizona, and Utah, and parts of Colorado, Wyoming, New Mexico.

I'm let in, no questions asked. It's harder to get into nightclubs than it is some countries. Mexico doesn't mind that I'm wearing flip-flops, or say, "Too many lads already."

On the other side of *la linea* is a bottleneck of traffic that clogs a dozen lanes; it's like a scene from a zombie movie where citizens fleeing a city are hemmed in by a government blockade. I walk past the cars and trucks to Zona Centro, to Avenida Revolucion. A caricature of the country, were I to buy even a quarter of that offered along the gauntlet of garishness I'd reach the end wearing cowboy boots, a summer dress, and a poncho, a necklace of seashells, a lucha libre mask, and a sombrero — and be arseholed on pina coladas, and high and hard on pills. On the side streets of Avenida Revolucion, as many pharmacies as there are bars, and arty cafes and record stores and microbreweries, and a buffet of street food at stalls and nooks in walls. I stroll around, feel as safe as I did in Los Angeles — safer than I did in Skid Row. At times it's been off-limits, but right now Tijuana is no more dangerous than Detroit. It's Mexico for beginners. A taste of something different, but not too much. A hamburger with chilli in it. So Americans drop in for the day to feast on tacos and tamales, and guzzle mega-sized margaritas while being serenaded by crooning mariachis.

A couple of day-trippers chat to me. I tell them I'm going to Brazil by bus and train, a boat or two.

They tell me I'm brave; their eyes say I'm stupid.

One, a rotund gum-chewer, says she buys a shot glass from each place she's been. Two hundred of each, she says; this the first from somewhere outside of the States. She asks, "Do you collect things from the places you go?"

"Yeah," I tell her, "STDs."

TIJUANA TO DIVISADERO

I'm in the back of a burgundy Toyota Yaris, a cooler of food and drink wedged between Monica and me. Genesis and Armida sit up front. The *chicas* chatter in Spanish. I understand almost nothing. I studied Spanish on the bus from Los Angeles to San Diego, but three hours — one of which I was asleep — wasn't enough time to become fluent. I met them in Tijuana. I said I was heading south to La Paz. They said they're from near there and were going back by car. "Did I want to join them?" asked Monica, the only one of the three who speaks any English.

Hell yeah.

We've gone quarters on the gas to cover the 1500 km between Tijuana and La Paz at the far south of Baja California, the finger-shaped peninsula that's twice the size of Belgium. The Pacific to the west. The Gulf of California to the east — a long slip of water between the peninsula and Mexico's mainland.

We ride out of Tijuana on a road beside the Pacific, past *playas* and *del mars* in a Mediterranean landscape. Through Ensenada, a low-key seaside town; through the rugged valleys, verdant vineyards, and boulder-strewn mountains of the Valle de Guadalupe. Then a narrow, hole-studded highway, winding and curving through brawny terrain, through a series of Sans: San Vicente, San Quintin, San Telmo. Trucks hurtle at us, thunder close by; the road barely wide enough to squeeze in a couple of passing vehicles. The girls cross their chests, whisper prayers. They're right to do so: beside the roadside carcasses of livestock picked clean are burnt-out chassis, victims of long-ago crashes. Names of the dead are spelt in stones on the canvases of barren hillsides.

For some the risk is multiplied a hundred-fold because they're not driving on these dangerous roads but cycling. Like the Australian couple I meet outside a store at one of the rare spots of life. Her eye is swollen from an insect bite. He's shaky — is recovering, he tells me, from a stay in hospital after suffering an intestinal infection. They've done well to get this far. Not from Tijuana; from Alaska, where their trip started. It will finish in Argentina.

"Christmas," he says, when I ask how long it will take.

I say, with surprise, "That's only a couple of months away."

But he doesn't mean *this* Christmas. "Christmas next year."

I'm glad I can't ride a bike; I'd no doubt stupidly attempt such a venture myself. I wouldn't, though, do it for a honeymoon, like this pair are. I reckon he had second thoughts about the marriage before the big day but left it too late to cancel. *I'll kill her off during the honeymoon,* he'll have said to himself. *I'll get to keep all the gifts from the wedding, and it's cheaper and less messy than getting a divorce. Cycle around Australia? No, she might survive. It has to be more extreme. I know: Alaska to Argentina; that she'll never survive.*

She'll struggle to survive even Baja California. Inland is desolate and primordial, emphatic, distorting emptiness. Dust and sand whirl around sporadic skeletal trees which wither from within baked earth that looks to have been blazed by blowtorch. Few and far between, the odd rustic ranch or stray home; lone souls wearing sombreros, chugging cervezas or snoozing. Through the Valle de los Cirios the dramatic desolation is decorated with millions of cacti, a spectrum of singular species casting strange shadows on the scalded terrain. Some like armoured cucumbers, others like cartoonish candelabra. Some thick and some thin, some soaring several stories. Some branch upwards, as if in worship of the sun; others lazily droop, as if sick of the heat. Some not cacti but cirio, a species found nowhere else in the world; from the seared soil they twist like surreal tentacles. All feels far-off and strange, totally foreign. Los Angeles and Tijuana were prelude; I feel my trip has begun.

On this Wild West stage are even some cowboys wearing spurred boots and ten-gallon hats, riding horses through the scorched wilderness. No Indians; bandits and cartels act the parts of bad guys in this show. Not cowboys keeping them in check, but police, military. Passing us on the road, and on patrol in the Sans, convoys of pickup trucks with swivel-mounted weaponry; those aboard wearing commando-type combat gear, eyes barely visible through balaclavas. We pass through multiple checkpoints manned by sullen soldiers in desert-camo. A dozen or more at each checkpoint — in Mexico, a couple might not be enough. Each time we're stopped, as every vehicle is. Questions are asked: *Where have you come from? Where are you going? Why?* Windows are peered through, a couple of times the trunk is opened, searched. Monica says, "They're looking for guns, drugs, things like that."

Repeated reminders that Mexico has its risks. Sufficient to scare off some. Based on fifth-hand anecdotes of all-out-warfare passed along like Chinese whispers, a whole country is painted with a bleak brush; only pockets, though, are affected. More tourists perish in plane crashes than die in Mexico. But people are wary of Mexico, think nothing of flying. What risks there are, I accept. Travel without risks isn't travel; it's a holiday — and if I wanted a holiday, I'd have gone to Majorca.

"Don't you miss home?" asks Monica when I tell her I'll be travelling for several months.

I tell her, "No, I miss the places I'm yet to go."

Exotic places like this feed my soul. The world is an all-you-can-eat buffet, and I'm a greedy bastard.

Another reason to travel for longer periods: in your absence, friends and family remember only your finest qualities; they forget your faults, forgive your wrongs. It's almost as if you've died. On your return, the red carpet is rolled, and you're treated like the resurrection. But you have to disappear for at least half a year to places considered dangerous. A month in the Maldives won't do.

At Guerro Negro we start to cross the peninsula, through the El Vizcaino Biosphere Reserve, Mexico's largest wildlife refuge. Eagles and coyotes and roadrunners: so they say, but I see none. Nothing stirs in the stark blue sky or the thorny scrub, among the cacti and heaps of rocks. In the distance the mountains of the Sierra de San Francisco; they're peppered with pictographs dating back millennia, when nude men painted other nude men on walls — an act that these days would get you jailed for gay-porn graffiti. To see the art requires a guide and permits. And it's a multi-day trek, camping in the wilderness; I'm equipped for neither. I travel light, have only 7 kg in my bag. I'm without all but the essentials — and also without several essentials: no towel, no trainers, no hairdryer. I do at least have footwear beyond flip-flops, having caved in to the demands of civilised society, which deems any man with his toes on show to be a hobo. A wise man packs hiking boots. A wise man I'm not: I've packed Chelsea boots.

On we drive: through San Ignacio, past ruined missions and mines, from the time when Spaniards came to seek their fortune in gold and favour with God; through valleys and over craggy hills, then skirting the Tres Virgenes volcanoes as we ride towards Santa Rosalia on the coast, from where we crest the coves and curves of the shore as we snake south. At La Paz — a scenic town by the sea — I catch a ferry across the tranquil, turquoise Gulf of California to Topolobampo, leaving behind Baja California.

A taxi and bus take me a hundred kilometres to El Fuerte, a *Pueblo Magico* — an honour granted to a hundred-or-so towns in Mexico deemed to be "magical". Squat, cared-for, colonial; its colours queer and bold: baby blues, quirky greens, blooming yellows. Buildings with pillars and arches and murals cluster around a leafy plaza: a bandstand and fountains, busts of beardy blokes. Bells clang from the pinkish steeple of the 19th-century church; couples canoodle on benches under white trunk palms; locals lazily lean, idle and natter; cowboys on horses circle. At such a place, that I sometimes stumble upon, I think I've found somewhere to settle. A lifetime plays out in my mind: a wife, a school for the kids, a spot in the cemetery. Then Truman Show Syndrome sinks in: the feeling that life is on a loop, that every day's the same, the same as every other — and I move on.

At the edge of town is a train station. A straggle of people along a platform that's more of a sidewalk, mongrels begging and barking at cows. No ticket office nor toilet; no one seems to work here. A four-carriage yellow-and-green train comes to a halt: the Ferrocarril Chihuahua al Pacifico, bound 700 km north-east to Creel through the canyons and mountains of the Sierra Madre Occidental. I climb aboard, buy a ticket from the conductor. Foreigners are few, many frightened off by the US-issued warning against travel in this area. In the wilds of canyon country there are places aplenty for *banditos* to spring from. And this is Narcoland. These canyons are strategic to the cartels. The climate is perfect for cultivation, the terrain is difficult to police, and it's not far from America. As protection, Khaki-wearing security patrol the train, rifles at the ready.

We set off through remote plains green with cacti and trees, ride past the rusted remains of carriages and locomotives, past haring pickup trucks that hurtle by in mists of dust, past glassy lakes and boulders as large as bungalows, and cross lofty bridges over rocky, crinkled riverbeds. Then into the mountains, slithering through like a serpent; a circuitous passage the only one the terrain permits.

The rear of the train is open-sided; I ask the conductor if it's ok to stand there.

He says no, but winks twice as he says it.

So I stand there, among sacks of corn, watch the track unravel behind like the tail of the train. I breathe the mountain freshness and listen to the clanking, rhythmic, drumming soundtrack of wheels on rails. The track is at times stuck on shelves slashed into mountainsides. Sheer drops, dizzying heights. Pine-scented forests at the peaks; the breeze rustles the trees, perfumes the air. Into shady ravines with soaring rockfaces textured like the scales of a beast, close enough to touch, asking to be stroked; and through tunnels short and long, some spaced only seconds apart: eighty-six in total. Bridges? Thirty-seven. An extraordinary engineering endeavour and it explains why it took so long to construct: completed in 1961; started at the turn of that century. The project was abandoned several times, deemed impossible.

As well as nature, stray signs of life: solitary houses framed by stone walls, holed linen strung on lines, smoking chimneys. There a fellow riverside, panning for silver, perhaps gold. There one lost in the wilds, walking, wandering; though likely not lost at all: his map the trees, the rocks, the rivers. In sloping woodlands smatterings of rudimentary settlements, bumpkins colourful in clothes and character. Women bent-over scrubbing laundry; others sat like sages, stories written in their wrinkles. Flower-patterned headscarves, flowing pleated skirts. Fingers working deftly: dolls and bowls, beads and baskets — woven or carved, created with care. Some at shacks beside the track, selling if the train comes to a stop, which we do at not only stations but at passenger requests — like we're a bus not a train.

At one stop, grills on top of oil drums, *gorditas* with a dozen types of fillings. "*Burro?*" the seller suggests.

Yeah, I tell her. I like beef.

It tastes odd. I enter *burro* into my Spanish-English dictionary app: donkey.

At a later stop a man boards holding a cassette player and a maraca: he twirls along the aisle, shakes the maraca to a folksy tune, does a half-arsed shuffle to the beat. A toothless semi-smile doesn't disguise his embarrassment. The passengers are just as embarrassed. Each hand over a few pesos to put it to an end. A few pesos is nothing, yet still too much.

At Divisadero I disembark. A dozen metres from the track is a vertigo-inducing, forbidding expanse. The earth cracks right open, plumbs 2000-plus metres. The *Barrancas del Cobre*. The Copper Canyon. To look should be enough, but it's not. There's a zip line; I sign up. Why, I don't know, because I'm not an extreme person. I've never skydived, nor bungee jumped. Given a choice between swimming with sharks or watching paint dry, I'll be down B&Q to stock up on Dulux. The need to scare oneself, I've never understood. A symptom, I suppose, of life being too comfortable. It's a modern phenomenon: after a week of dodging dinosaurs, cavemen didn't spend their weekend spelunking. It's not death that I fear, but disfigurement or losing a limb. Life's tough enough without being a legless munter. I have travel insurance but don't need to check the small print to know this won't be covered. Being the cheapest policy, I'm covered for nothing beyond walking (only then if I wear a crash helmet).

After I sign up — a disclaimer says they're not to blame for "accidental death" — I walk to the edge and peer over. Wind swirls riotously upwards from the abyss. My gut churns, and my heart thumps, as I stare down at the foot of the canyon that I picture stained with brains and blood. I go to the toilet, inside a cubicle: head in hands, full-on panic.

But I'll do it.

A local and his kid, aged about ten, are with me. The kid wears a Spiderman t-shirt. I wear all black like I've come to live out a Batman fantasy. We're given gloves and a helmet, a harness and a backpack. Then a guy gives us a demo on a line a metre off the ground. He shows us how to hang and position our weight, where to put our hands and not to place our head, and covers hand signals, braking, etc. Important information given in Spanish, half translated. There's no trial run on the demo line: Straight in at the deep end. Peter Parker has no nerves, goes first. I half hope he falls off midway across; that would be a get-out-of-jail-free card for me: "I can't do it now. It wouldn't feel right. I'll go to the cafe and get his Dad a Snickers."

As he's done it, I'll have to. I'm representing my country whether they like it or not — and let's be honest, they would rather I wasn't. Adrenaline skyrockets as I'm hooked to the line. My legs go numb, my ears ring. *I'm Batman*, I tell myself, *off to save the world*. But I know the truth: I'm not Batman; I'm barely even a man. I await a countdown, ready myself; then without warning, I'm pushed. At what feels like warp speed I'm on my way, excreting pitches higher than I have done since I was six. I scream, yell every curse: ". . . bloodyfuckingbastardbollocks . . ."

I slam into the buffer, rebound backwards. My eyes are watery from the wind in my face. I wipe them dry, don't want Spiderkid to think I'm crying.

"Enjoy?" asks the guy, as he unhooks me from the line.

"Yeah," I say, only half lying. I think I did; I can't remember.

I've had my thrill. I'm happy to call it a day. But there's nowhere to go but onwards, downwards. Not once more, but six more times; on lines that range in length from 200 to 1100 metres. As well as zip lines to deal with, precarious pathways perched on the sides of steep slopes; little in the way of barriers, no nets to catch me should I slip. And also rickety bridges: a plank of wood, a rope each side to hold on to. They sway with the wind and bounce because Spiderkid uses them as a trampoline. *Push him off*, says the devil in me. But I reason myself out of it: I'd also have to push off the witnesses. A judge might believe the wind blew one off, but not three.

By the last line, the longest, I'm into it. "Na, na, na, na, na, na, na, na, na, na, na, na, Batmaaaaaan!" I shout mid-flight. Then I see the guy signal to brake. I think that's what he signals, anyway. He's far off, and I'm at speed. He may be making a wanker gesture. I brake. Too hard. I stop short, slide back, back, back. Hundreds of metres from the end, suspended and swaying, I feel sick. There's no rescue. I turn around backwards, then hand over hand on the wire, inch myself slowly, slowly along.

I'm spent come the end. I feel like I've shot a month's

worth of loads in a single sordid afternoon. Unlike a curtains-drawn wankathon, though, I'm glad I did it. Fail to face fears, and they hold power over you, like a monster under your bed; when you face them, the monster morphs into a puppy.

BATOPILAS

"Batopilas is narco-run, belongs to the Sinaloa Cartel," said the owner of my hotel in Creel, 45 km from Divisadero. "In the canyons around are hidden fields of opium and marijuana; they grow drugs there, bring them through Creel to distribute."

"Killings?" I queried. "Kidnappings?"

He said not. "Trouble isn't good for business." He also said that it's not a bad thing for the area: no thieves, no drunks. People don't dare to misbehave. "And it brings money into the community; many locals are involved."

"But the police, the army?"

"That's just for show," he said. "The cartels operate with impunity. Mexico is a narco-state; from top to bottom people profit from drugs. It's not in the interest of the police and army to cause problems. The system works, so they let it work."

Now I'm bound for Batopilas at the bottom of the *Barrancas del Cobre.* The battered minivan is packed, goods as well as people. No one wears a seatbelt because there are none. It's a 140-km drive to what feels like the core of the earth. Rock has been crudely cut or blown through to create the thin road that ribbons into the canyon. Barely a stretch is straight. We slalom upwards then downwards, upwards then downwards, hugging the very edge of sheer cliffs — barriers wrecked by accidents or rockslides. Half the road is at points impassable — too many rocks, too large — and at one section a hastily-made slip road. Nature, angered by the incursion, is reasserting its authority; this road is but a brief irritant, assured to be reclaimed.

On some slopes maize gleams golden under the sun; on others sinuous footpaths to lonesome buildings or to seemingly nowhere at all. On one runs a lean, dark male; he wears a bright blouse and skirt-like white wrap. A Tarahumara, the region's indigenous inhabitants. One hundred thousand is the estimate, but with their nomadic tendencies, and no official census, no one really knows. They live in these canyons, widely scattered and secluded, in primitive shelters and hobbit-like abodes. The arrival of the Spanish *conquistadores* centuries ago saw their ancestors take refuge where it was too rugged for others to venture. They chose flight over fight — a fight they would have lost. And here they've remained, preferring free-range living over life in a city coop.

They like to run, and run far. One hundred kilometres in a single journey isn't uncommon. Not just one or two, the cream of the crop; any able-bodied Tarahumara, from teenagers to old-timers. So next time a showoff boasts on Facebook that they've run a marathon, tell them: "Let us know when you've done two in a row, you lazy bore."

Tarahumaras actually ran the marathon in the 1968 Olympics; after finishing nowhere of note, they said it was because the race was too short. They're a link to our past: In the time before spears and arrows, animals were chased to their death, utilising humans' superpower: sweating. Because animals that don't sweat (which is the vast majority of animals) must cease running when they overheat, for long distances humans can outrun almost any of our four-legged brethren — not me, though; the only thing I run is out of breath.

We can learn from the Tarahumaras: Heart disease and high blood pressure are almost unknown among them. Diabetes? Cancers? Not an issue. Nor are crime, child abuse, domestic violence. And their world includes no suicide, no murder. Their biggest problem is narcos seizing their territory. Or forcing them to be drug mules: Give one a backpack filled with drugs and tell him to run with it to America; if he politely refuses, kill one of his family, then ask him again. Some don't need to be forced: Their people starving, they sign up voluntarily. For a drop-off over the border, $1000.

At the foot of the canyon is Batopilas, a stuck-in-time riverside *pueblo* strung along a single street. It's so neat it could almost be fake, a set for a film. Prim-and-proper pastel-coloured buildings with wooden shutters and doors; flower-spruced balconies, bougainvillea in blossom. A pretty plaza: antique lampposts and decorative benches, a silver statue of a man with a mule, an ornate wooden bandstand; the ground furnished with yellow leaves from grand, shady trees; dogs dozing, sunning themselves, and children playing, dancing, preening; smiling at the youth, fellas of an age to have specks of silver under their nails.

Mining paid for its finery — at least at first it did. In 1632 rich veins of silver were discovered in these canyons. Fortunes were made, the town flourished — it was the second place in Mexico to have electricity. The silver dried up early in the 20th century, and the town began to decline. Then seeds took over from silver. Seeds of opium, of marijuana. And there are signs of suspicion that this sweet place is but a comely charade. Flashy pickups speed by, half a dozen stone-faced ruffians stood in the back; into the rear of some, sealed sacks are loaded. And there's activity at an unmarked building beside the *Presidencia Municipal*, a government building that borders the plaza: thickset people in and out; guns and radios but no uniforms. And on a lane off the plaza I come upon a thuggish hombre sat with an AK-47 on his lap. We make eye contact, and I don't know what else to do but say good afternoon; so that's what I do, then walk on.

I stand out for sure; like if a Mexican arrived in Emmerdale, walked into The Woolpack wearing a sombrero and said, "*Una margarita, por favor*"; the locals would gossip as to who he was, what he was doing there.

Should I have come?

Yes. Dare to roll the dice, I say; risk a one for a six. The scenery en route and this town are like no other I've seen. And it's a story to tell. Life should be about stories. "So, anyway, this one time in Mexico a narco shot me . . ." What a shame, what a waste, to be sat in the old farts' home and have little to reminisce, be short on tales to tell.

"Grandpa," says Little Johnny, "tell me about your life."

"I worked in an office for fifty years. At weekends I went shopping, I watched TV, I drank beer."

"Is that it?"

"Err, let me think . . . oh, and I married your nan . . . and nine years later we divorced."

"Anything else?"

"No, that's all, basically."

"Oh," says Little Johnny, frowning. "Will my life be like that?"

"Your life, Little Johnny, will be different. You can be anything, do anything. You can be a pirate if you want. A princess if you prefer."

Then they hit eleven, start at big-boy school, and the bubble is popped. Dreams of being an astronaut are no longer tolerated. "Be an accountant, Little Johnny; that's where the money is, that's what pays the mortgage."

And so it starts: A lifetime of slaving and saving for a life that never gets lived.

That said, I'm not on a suicide mission; so I sit in the plaza with a book, give the narcos no reason to kill me.

After a while a bloke introduces himself as Rafael, says he runs the museum, a one-room affair on the plaza. "And this is the mayor," he says, pointing to a man in jeans and shirt, sat on the next bench, typing on his phone. The mayor looks over and smiles; we exchange *mucho gustos*.

Rafael says I should go hiking: "There's an old silver mine you can see. A guy I know can show you the way."

The guy is Lupe; he wears Wranglers and a Stetson and carries a knife. He looks the part — whereas with my Chelsea boots and skinny jeans I look like I've got lost on the way to a gig. He also looks his age — all seventy-two years of them.

We zigzag up an incline. The scree path is only a foot's

width. Cacti line the way, spiky sentinels guarding the riches; they stab and prick my clumsy hands. What seem solid rocks give way when I grip them, and my feet slip and slide. These Chelsea boots, I worry, will be the end of me. A few times Lupe reaches his hand out for me to hold, to help me navigate particularly precarious sections. Dressed as a cowboy and holding my hand, I almost make a joke about *Brokeback Mountain*. He might take offence, though, let go of my hand, and I'll die — so I settle for a quiet giggle to myself.

After an hour, when Batopilas is far below, comes an opening in the canyon. A barred entrance that looks like the gate to hell. Lupe yanks it open. We enter the pitch-black passage, are swallowed by darkness. I fumble my way forward, feel a way along. The walls look as though clawed — chisel marks made by men of a past time. Some found their fortune; some their death. What a place to work, to die. So bleak. Even if they put beanbags and a ping-pong table in a mine, I'd refuse to work in one. I'd rather work in a brothel, have my rectum mined. The crunch of our steps breaks the eerie silence of all else; then in the spooky still- ness, a sound of sinister portent: Bats fly at us. Fearing they'll bite, I cover my face. Lupe laughs at them — or maybe he's laughing at me. He starts to talk, but as he speaks in Spanish, I understand scarcely a word. Explain- ing, probably, the history of the mine, or warning me about a large hole I'm about to fall down. I ask to turn back: It's a real deal mine, the same now as it was then — when safety wasn't in the dictionary. I can't risk getting trapped with supplies so minimal: we have only half a bottle of Coke. The key for my hotel has a leather keyring; I could maybe suck a few calories from that. He has a knife, so is less worried; he could live off me for a month.

After a nap, I'm back in the plaza. Nothing else to do but sit. No Starbucks. No Netflix. No porn. It's like the past. The past was shit. Seeing me there, an elderly woman named Señora Monse invites me for dinner at her home: a wood-beamed, low-lying ceiling; religious imagery hanging on the orange walls. A bowl of red chillies at the centre of the dining table, surrounded by a jumble of odds and ends, like a display at a thrift store. Beside the table are a cat and a bulging-eyed Chihuahua; she feeds them, and also a cripple out front, who slurps down a bowl of soup.

She serves me rice, peas, and beef, with a side plate of tortillas as thick as naans. We chat as I eat; at one point I ask her about that unmarked building, the suspicious comings and goings. She shifts uncomfortably, mumbles a few syllables — the equivalent of "No comment." — then changes the subject, pointing at a wedding photo: fifty-four years ago, she tells me; they married in the church beside the plaza.

Freshly-picked grapefruit for dessert. She then hands me a mug of tea; leaves float in it. She says, "This is what the Tarahumara drink."

It might save me buying any more bus or train tickets. By the end of the week I'll have run to Rio.

As we've dined, people have come back and forth through her house, between the plaza and her overgrown garden. Most are clad in old-style clothing. It feels like a portal to another century. They pay me no attention as they pass, not even a look. Señora Monse speaks their language, which sounds like nothing I've heard before. Not the structure nor tones of those spoken in Europe or Asia. Now a woman walks in from the yard, then walks out with a bag of salt.

"Who's that?" I ask. "And what's she doing in your yard?"

"She's a Tarahumara; she's staying there tonight with her family. I have a couple of rooms out there."

"How many people are staying?"

"I'm not sure. Twelve, I think. People come and go."

"You know all of them?"

"Not all, no."

She runs, it seems, a kind of shelter, providing temporary accommodation to Tarahumaras. She tells me they sometimes steal the blankets from the rooms. "But I don't mind," she says. "If they take them, it's because they need them, and are ashamed to ask if they can have one. They need them more than me."

I give her some cash when I leave — for the meal, for what she does for others. It doesn't lessen my guilt when I later get into my double bed. I could have invited a Tarahumara or twelve to join me.

PALENQUE

Five hours by bus from Batopilas to Chihuahua; from there a through-the-night eighteen-hour journey to Mexico City. Before boarding, airport-style security: IDs checked and bodies frisked, luggage scanned and searched. The driver locked in his cabin, the glass tinted and bulletproof — shielded from bandits and the stink of chow mein, which several passengers brought on board on paper plates from a cafe at one stop. I'd rather have sat beside someone with a knife than a plate of chow mein. I had a seat next to the bog; if we were ambushed, I could have used it as a panic room. I'd have taken my chances, however, because the toilet was vile, the toxic whiff like a soiled diaper on a warm day. Drop-down screens with volume dialled to granny-friendly prevented sleeping. Too large and sprawling to comprehend, I skipped through the capital. I'd not have scratched the surface of, and didn't have the enthusiasm for, the 21-million-person megalopolis — the second largest city in the Americas after Brazil's Sao Paulo. A dozen hours more from

Mexico City to the jungled humid south, which could be another country to the north, its desert and canyons.

At Palenque, near the border with Guatemala, the green peels away to reveal a Mayan metropolis mysteriously abandoned a millennium ago. Reclaimed by the jungle, buried and hidden, forgotten. Then, in the 1700s, rediscovered. A page of history thought tippexed has since been excavated: finely-sculpted structures with names to seduce Indiana: Tomb of the Red Queen, Temple of the Foliated Cross. Palenque prospered from 200 to 900 AD, at the peak of the Mayan's powers when they ruled a third of Mesoamerica: south-east Mexico, all of Belize and Guatemala, and portions of Honduras and El Salvador. A 2000-year-old civilisation, the Mayans had a complex language and accurate calendar. Geography, though, not a strength: they were blind to Europe, Africa, Asia; of their existence, not even a whisper of a rumour. No atlas, and also without the wheel and metal tools. That they built a place like Palenque without a spanner or a wheelbarrow is extraordinary.

Stepped pyramids are Palenque's showpieces. Now grey but for moss and grass, in their heyday they were vivid blues and reds and were adorned with stucco and artistic glyphs. Priests off their face on peyote would stand atop the pyramids preaching, their visions taken as the truths of the gods. Those gods needed payment and were paid in human blood. The doomed were decapitated. Or were stripped and painted blue, spreadeagled on a stone altar; a priest then sliced a flint blade into their chest and seized their still-beating bloody heart. Sometimes the corpse would be skinned, and the priest would wear the skin and do a little dance. Now people swarm up the structures; sweat streams from beneath their I-Love-Mexico baseball caps. On one a guide verbally downloads Wikipedia's Palenque article onto a baffled Korean; the facts sound somewhat embellished: three times he mentions asteroids. On another is a woman with a baby in her arms: "Boo, boo, bedgy wedgy, uh, da, ba ba do wa." — talk used for infants and animals and foreigners that can't speak Spanish. At the top of the Temple of the Count, I survey my minions below as they stand snapping themselves. Bless their little souls; as if anyone wants to look at a photo of *them*. One seems to be taking notes; to write a book about his vacation probably — the pinnacle of narcissism. I shout down at him: "Slave, fetch me a Sprite." He ignores my order. I'd dock his wages if I were paying him any; as I'm not, I'll gift his cock to the gods. Last time I gave them one, three weeks later it rained — proof that the gods exist.

The nine-tier Temple of Inscriptions is the standout. Within is one of the most important archaeological discoveries of the 20th century: a vaulted chamber containing the crypt of Pakal, Palenque's greatest guv'nor. He took the throne when he was twelve. A twelve-year-old these days can't even work at Tesco. The carvings on Pakal's sarcophagus caused debate. Out-there theorists believe they depict an astronaut. Others think Pakal was a martian deified by the Maya while on a visit to earth. Some swear the sarcophagus itself is an ancient spaceship. I see a replica of the sarcophagus at the on-site museum, and I understand the outlandish interpretations: Pakal does appear to be piloting something futuristic. It doesn't mean the guy was Spock, though. More likely is that the sculptor was tripping on mescaline.

Ceramics and trinkets make up the majority of the museum. From Maya & Spencer, probably, but an elaborate narrative is always woven — historians have bills to pay. The mass-produced bric-a-brac of today will in the future be ascribed meaning when in truth it was tat gifted at Christmas. That will be forgotten centuries from now, and our now will be a source of fascination. A selection of figurines catch my eye; they show how nobles mutilated themselves to flaunt their rank: tattooing their faces, filing their front teeth into a T-shape, shaping their skulls to look like a cob of corn. Would have been easier to wear a badge. Zero books on display; the Spanish burnt them. Only four survive from 2000 years of Mayan literature, and they reside in overseas museums. Millennia from now only four books from Western civilisation might remain, and posterity may judge us on them. Three of those four could be mine; the other Kim Kardashian's autobiography.

Sods they were, complete *bastardos*, but the Spanish weren't to blame for the collapse of Palenque; by their arrival, it was buried under a layer of green. Not only Palenque but also other Mayan cities like Copan and Tikal; their demise is a puzzle yet to be solved. The Spanish, though, did snuff out the Mayans, who until their arrival survived on a smaller scale for 600 years after the fall of their great cities. The Aztecs, who bossed Mesoamerica when the Spanish arrived, were also annihilated. Twenty-seven years after Columbus discovered the New World in 1492, conquistador Hernan Cortes came in search of riches and souls. He stumbled upon the Aztec capital Tenochtitlan, a place of palaces and pyramids, home to a quarter of a million — many more than Madrid. The emperor

Montezuma mistook Cortes for an incarnation of Quetzal-coatl and offered gifts of gold. In 1521, two years after arriving, Cortes repaid the kindness with conquest. The Aztecs far outnumbered the Spanish, but were outplayed and outgunned — and succumbed to smallpox and measles and other Old World diseases. On went the Spanish, steamrollering southwards through Mesoamerica, and north into what is now the US. All was razed, rebuilt in the style of the Spanish, the stones of the old reused for the new. And the land was renamed: *Nueva Espana* — which is like Steve calling his child New Steve.

Sympathy for the Mayans and Aztecs, though, would be misplaced: they ascended on conquering those weaker, on slavery and human sacrifice. What they reaped, they sowed. And the Spanish themselves capitulated after three centuries. Civilisations are sandcastles. Time is the sea. What was is not now, and what's now is not what will be. Everything thought certain and stable today will fade, to one day be mused over in museums by people saying what fools we were, what folly we believed — like the world ending on December 21st 2012. The glyphs at Palenque sparked that hoopla. Some were so sure the world would end that they bought one-way tickets to Mexico and sat on these pyramids meditating as they waited for worldwide armageddon.

While the world didn't end in 2012, the people of Palenque were right that *they* wouldn't see in 2013. Palenque, though, had a good run: 700 years. New York is not yet 400. And the Mayans and Aztecs aren't entirely reduced to rubble and tales; their DNA lives on: tens of millions of descendants in Guatemala, Mexico, and Belize.

Ruins seen, I take a tour of the jungle around. The trees are Tolkien, several stories high; the flora moist and dense. I duck under branches, push aside vines — except for one that's too tempting: "Ahheyaheaaaaaa." I nearly smack into a tree. A German does. He wears flip-flops, struggles with the terrain. What a fool he is, wearing flip-flops in the jungle. I consider lending him one of my Chelsea boots, but no, he must learn his lesson.

Julio — the guide, built like a bear — talks to us about the trees: ". . . There's a cacao tree . . . That one's avocado . . ." He points at one and says, "You can hug this tree if you want."

I hug the tree; I ask if there's a health benefit.

"No."

He says next to one with a spiky trunk, "Be very careful. This tree is very, very dangerous."

If he's that concerned, it could be deadly. Poison passed through the spikes, perhaps, resulting in paralysation, followed by torturous months before you breathe your final breath.

"What happens if you touch it?" I ask, expecting a response scarier than a snuff movie.

"You get a headache," he says, "and it lasts for thirty minutes."

Worse is the plant that if consumed constricts your throat. Spaniards fed it to slaves to silence them when whipped. Some suffocated.

Spotting a mound of termites, Julio asks if we want to eat one. He lets several crawl onto his hand; I pick one off, pop it in my mouth. It tastes earthy, bitter, rank. I ask if he has any other flavours.

He hasn't.

He says sometimes he has a termite burrito.

They're so tiny; he'd need to put in a lot. I ask how many.

"About a thousand."

When we stop to drink from a stream, Julio calls to the monkeys: "Ooo ah ooo ah ah." A guy asks what other animals there are. Julio says armadillos, scorpions, tarantulas, toucans, ocelots, jaguars, snakes. The most dangerous, usually found north of here, but they're known to stray far and wide, much feared, infamous for attacking without provocation, and responsible for thousands of deaths a year, is the American. If one approaches, don't climb a tree or play dead — this will anger the beast; it will likely shoot you. Feed it a donut instead, and while it's distracted, sprint to safety, zigzagging.

Later I'm sat outside my bare-bones mouldy room: jungle on all sides, cloaked by a curtain of darkness. Dastardly creatures — at least four legs too many — make dives of death at the lightbulb overhead, and whining mosquitoes harass me, hell-bent on a donation to their bloody cause. A high-pitched symphony sounds, and from a distance too close for comfort, guttural, roaring howls — a cross between Chewbacca and Drogon. It's howler monkeys, one of the world's loudest animals. They have only one setting — howling — so I can't be sure if they're sounds of love or war. I'd prefer not to scrap or shag, but at heart I'm a lover not a hater. And if I had to have sex with an animal — under duress, for example, or as, say, a dare, or because I was lonely or bored — I suppose a monkey is the one. In this situation — far from home, alone in the jungle — society might be sympathetic, and a judge might accept it as extenuating circumstances: "We all have needs," he'd say to the crowded courtroom. They would, though, expect me to hold out more than one day. Less than a week makes a man seem too keen, makes it seem like that's the reason he went to the jungle.

The room reminds me of one I once had in Thailand, and as I try to sleep I'm struck by a troubling flashback: I came out the shower one morning whistling *Wonderwall* and noted something strange hanging from under a painting angled above the door at the foot of the bed. *What is that?* I jumped on the bed to peer behind the painting. *That,* I saw, was a coiled snake. I ran out the door squealing, wearing only a towel. I used sign language to communicate the situation to the manager. His look said I was a wimp, that I was scared of an itsy-bitsy snake. My sign language must not have adequately made the point that it was almost an anaconda because three seconds after swaggering into my room he ran out. His squeals made mine sound like Pavarotti. He sheepishly returned with his pal, each carrying a broomstick. They knocked the snake from its perch and chased it from the room. It slithered into the bushes. I don't know how that snake got there — the cleaner is the prime suspect; an act of revenge — but I do know that my door was locked from 10pm the night before. It was there all night, a metre from my bed. Since then I've always cleaned my room before the cleaner comes.

PALENQUE TO GUATEMALA CITY

A man the size of two men, biceps as thick as my neck. He's at a desk, on a chair large enough to be a throne, staring at me squirm on the sofa. My butt is sticky with sweat from the faux leather. His henchman, who forced me to come to this dingy room, is stood beside him, doubling the sullen eyes on the prey. Door closed. Blinds drawn.

"Pay," he says. His expression emotionless, the perfect poker face.

I say, "I'm not paying."

The more I protest, the less English he speaks, the more bullying his attitude. He soon speaks only Spanish.

I glance at the door: I could make a run for it. But the door may be locked, and I don't know where I can run to. I'm in the middle of nowhere, on the border between Mexico and Guatemala. And on the other side of the door are men with guns.

The room grows smaller with each second, slowly

crushing my defiance. But I have some left: "I'm not paying," I say again.

He scowls, says, "*No pagas, no te vas.*" Don't pay, don't leave. Said with an absoluteness that permits no argument.

Gatekeeper is used as a metaphor; he's a literal one, in charge of this gate out of Mexico. He won't let me leave until I've paid £20 for a tourist permit. But I paid when I entered the country. He knows I've paid: it's impossible to enter Mexico without paying. Under the pretence of officialdom, I'm being mugged. He knows I know there's nothing I can do about it. He's the judge, the jury. If I continue to refuse, he'll tell me to sod off. It took me four hours to get here. To get to another border crossing, I'll have to return to Palenque and travel four-plus hours south from there — where I may have the same issue. Or he'll plant drugs on me. Not a sizeable amount — it wouldn't be believable for me to traffic against the northbound tsunami — but a gram or two he could get away with.

"Can I pay by card?" I ask.

"No."

"Can I get a receipt?"

"No."

Cash only: Confirmation that it's a con.

I pay. I've no choice.

"*Feliz Navidad,*" I say, as I stand to leave, smiling as I wish him a Merry Christmas.

He looks at me like I've spat on him.

As I walk out the door, I add: "Twunt." A safe insult: sounds offensive, but he can't be certain that it is.

I quick-walk just in case; past pickup trucks with cargoes of people, past loiterers primed to prey. Over the line into

Guatemala, it's time to do, not dwell. The country behind is dumped, forgotten in favour of the new, its flirting and promises. Fickle like that are travellers, promiscuous.

From the border at El Ceibo, a minivan to Flores in the north of Guatemala. The station there is a frenetic jigsaw, its many pieces in motion. Dust rises from wheels and footfall; people cover their face, cough and splutter. Some spit, some piss on walls. Shoeshiners struggle for silk purses from pigs' ears; the shinees on wooden thrones, paupers playing princes. A guard outside a shop — one selling day-to-day items not diamonds — shotgun slung about his neck. Pilfer a pack of Oreos: BANG. You're dead. I've no such protection. It's a sad state of affairs when you're worth less than a pack of Oreos. Cries of "*Aqua, aqua. Fruta, fruta.*" Others stick their head in minivans to peddle socks and batteries, medicines and fireworks. Someone's selling a framed picture of a woman posing sexily on all fours, a waterfall photoshopped in the background.

I board a minivan bound for Sayaxche, south of here on my screenshot of a map of Guatemala. The distance on the map isn't far, but the terrain between there and here is unknown. How long it will take, I've no idea: an hour or seven or twelve. I don't mind. Days like these on the road are some of the best on a trip like this; thinking and observing, channel-surfing, catching glimpses, flashes, bits. I'll ride until darkness draws down a veil, then bed down until sunrise. Where I don't know; I'll deal later with detail. No need to stress: always a town of some sort or size, always a hotel, a store. I won't sleep on the streets. I won't starve.

The van is buggered. One window cracked like a snowflake, stuck with sellotape. Strapped to the roof are suitcases soiled by the decades; also bicycles and sacks of all sorts, tied tenuously in place. My bag is on my lap. Any bigger and it would need to go on top, exposed to thieves, to the elements. It's the litmus test for those who say they travel light: if you're not comfortable with your bag on your lap for hours, it's not light. Seats soon full. Plastic stools put in the aisle — soon full too. Several stand. One with a chicken; a live one, its feet and beak tied. Quetzales go out through windows; plates of tacos come in. Others buy fried slices of bananas or strawberries coated in chocolate. Crumbs tumble from mouths, adding to those already on the seats and floor. I'd pity the person who had to clean this van — if such a person existed. We cruise about town with the door open, scouting for extras. Somehow squeezed in, another four children and three chickens. A butt nudges my face; a baby sucks a breast, close enough for me to suck the other. A girl sings Christmas-sounding songs. I'd prefer a Christmas-sounding silence. All but me are locals. My blue eyes give away that I'm not of this parish, that I'm a wanderer wandering. But no one's bothered about my presence.

I'm taking a locals' *colectivo* — rather than a tourist shuttle — to hide in plain sight. Desperadoes, I reason, are less likely to hijack a minivan of paupers than a busload of foreigners. Still, to be on the safe side, I have money stashed all over: various pockets and parts of my bag — even down my sock. A thief might empty my pockets and take my bag, but steal my socks, surely not. Some of it is now dirty money; it will need to be laundered with Vanish. Paranoid? Perhaps. But with reason: Guatemala is ranked as one of the twenty-five most dangerous countries in the world. It's fifth for gun-related deaths per 100,000 people. Weapons are abundant; gangs operate unchecked. An assassin can be hired for less than £100. Police are overwhelmed: A force of 30,000 for a population of seventeen million. 90% of homicides remain unsolved. The past scars the present: endemic violence a legacy of the civil war that ravaged Guatemala from 1960 to 1996. Torturing, kidnapping, murdering. The police, the military, the government as guilty as anyone. At the end of the war, an amnesty was granted for even the worst crimes. No one was accountable.

As bad as it is in Guatemala, it's far worse in Honduras — twice the murder rate of Guatemala. And El Salvador — three times. I'll have to pass through one of those on my route south through Central America. Choices, choices.

Out of Flores a tropical landscape unblemished, as green and wild as Mother intended. The largest settlements barely stretch back from the road they straddle. Hardly a building is higher than a storey. Huts for homes, shacks for shops. Walls of wood; roofs of steel, of thatch. Some are concrete, bland and grey as the day they were built. Homes to be lived in not looked at. To me, these places are a black and white outline; but to the resident, intricate and coloured. Each of the people are as complex as you or I, engaged in a struggle to achieve something. Or to simply survive. But what can I see in a passing second but that which is obvious, and what is obvious is poverty. More like India than Mexico. Mexico was more like the US than here. Breadline living, basic as can be, is the norm for Guatemalans: 55% live in poverty; 29% in extreme poverty, on less than £2 a day.

The road dead-ends at the bend of a river, the Rio de la Pasion. "Coban?" I ask the driver, the next town on the map.

He points over the river.

A motor canoe ferries me across. On the other side is Sayaxche, a town of dusty roads running at right angles, of bumpkin commotion and bumbling disorder. Vans come and go; none set for Coban — their destination known via a sign in the windscreen or the shout of the driver. There's no ticket booth, no timetables. Purgatorial waiting ensues. It could be an hour, could be three. I may end up sleeping in Sayaxche. This is travel: A series of faltering transitions. Uncertainty is what you sign up for.

After a time, a driver breaks from yelling a destination that begins with R to ask me where I'm going.

"Coban," I tell him.

He doesn't understand.

I tell him again.

He still doesn't understand but tells me to get in the van.

I get in.

Coban doesn't begin with R, but I don't have to go to Coban. What is it to me but a strange name on a map? On this journey of long-distance aimlessness, wherever I am is where I'm meant to be. Each place is as worthy as any other. So on I go, on the move towards an uncertain destination, a destination that's only a destination until it's reached; then it becomes a departure.

After two hours the van stops at a crossroads. The driver tells me to get out.

"Here?" I ask, gesturing at nothing. We're not in a town, not even a village.

"*Si*," he says, and more I don't comprehend.

I get out, hope the part I didn't understand was that vans to Coban, or to somewhere, will drive by, pick me up.

A van does soon come, from the direction the previous one sped off to. It stops for me. "Coban?" I ask.

He nods. I jump on board.

It's packed beyond capacity, of course. This van also has a cracked window; the difference is that it's the windscreen, the width of it. The interior panels are missing; the sliding door at times slides itself open. The only thing in good shape are the speakers — blasting eighties synth-pop. The driver's in a rush — they all are. He tries to overtake a truck on a bend, failing to see another oncoming at full throttle. Catastrophe narrowly avoided. He does the same again at the next bend. And this with a phone to his ear. The woman beside me starts a conversation, asks me where I'm from, what I think of Guatemala. My review of Guatemala is a thumbs-up. It was either that or a thumbs-down. It's difficult to be nuanced with your thumbs.

This leg is on a remote stretch of road through Alta Verapaz, the greenest and wettest region in Guatemala, where on steep slopes sprout coffee and cardamom; through villages of indigenous communities: women wearing brightly-hued blouses, babies stashed in slings on backs. A man leads a mule laden with firewood. Livestock wanders loose. The road rises and falls as it passes the densely-forested mountainscape, summits masked by mist. The rain just falls, obscuring the driver's view; as does the steaming of the windows. With the rain, the steam, the crack, and the stickers of Christ, visibility is 10%. The relentless downpour drenches bedraggled villagers who trudge roadside through muddy puddles that are fast forming streams, turning crater-sized potholes into swimming pools. None of the villagers carries an umbrella; a few use bin bags as cagoules.

Coban is drab, of no note; and Salama, the next stop, nondescript if you're generous, dreadful if you're not. A place to come to go, and the next place to go is the capital: Guatemala City. A bus this time, not a minivan; a so-called "chicken bus", to be precise: a decades-old school bus, a hand-me-down from Big Bro up north. At the end of their shelf life in the States, they're sent south for a new lease of life as a psychedelic-painted death trap. Besides a coat of paint, this one's jazzed with cuddly toys and a sound system that puts to shame those in the Balearics. Eclectic playlist: sugary ballads to pulsing techno. Why bus drivers insist on playing dancefloor bangers, I don't know. No one on a bus wants to dance. Music should be the country's equivalent of Coldplay: subdued and forgettable. What they spent on the sound system they should have spent on the suspension: my organs are rearranged. School children weren't meant to be driven at such speed. Haste to race ahead of other buses — to be first to pick up passengers — and also to thwart attacks: Gangs MS-13 and Barrio 18 govern here. They enforce extortion schemes; charges levied per bus per week. Pay or die. Passengers are at risk as well, which is why the UK Government's official foreign travel advice for Guatemala includes: "Avoid travelling on public buses (repainted US school buses)."

The sun has set by the time I reach Guatemala City. A murder rate fifty times that of London. And even that is understated: The police don't count it as a homicide if a victim leaves the crime scene alive but later dies from the injuries. I want to hop on a bus to Antigua, 45 km away, but this is the northern bus terminal, and all the buses here go only north — where I've just come from. I ask at the information counter about hotels near the station. They say there are none, that I need to get a bus to the city centre. I board the bus they tell me to, the *Transurbano*; the others on board are mainly blokes, expressions chiselled to fuck-you. Scummy suburbs sprawl, dimly-lit shantytowns tacked onto slopes, run-down buildings, rusting vehicles. Heads pop up and peer, then quickly disappear, like urban whack-a-mole. Sinister weasels scuttle between cinder block boxes, skulk in the shadows. I'm close to panic: One of the deadliest cities in the world, and I'm riding a bus at night, no idea where I am.

Half an hour passes with me staring through the mucked window at signs that don't speak to me, thinking I can't get off here, or here, or here. I'm still hoping for a Starbucks or McDonald's — something that signals it's a safer spot than others — when the bus stops and everyone gets off. It's the last stop. No choice but to walk, but to where? Asking randoms where to go will show my hand, out me as lost and alone to them and anyone around. Fine in a rural town in the day, not in a homicide hotspot at night. If I hail a taxi, he'll ask *which* hotel, and I'll say *any* hotel, and he'll think I'm a mug ripe to rob. And he'd be right. So I stand on a corner and look up the four streets, assess which has the most life and walk down that one. I do the same again, and again, and again, follow the flow of people; past beat-up buildings and glowering doorways and gutters choked with garbage and shops that have their fronts barred like cells; past scraggy mutts and scrawny children in scruffed clothes, their glassy eyes focused on the faraway. On one of many checks over my shoulder, I see a guy who was on the bus; I cross the road, quicken, zigzag. Street stalls take up a chunk of the sidewalk, causing knocks and bumps. I brace for a brush of the pocket, the sly steal; ball my hand in a fist, ready to strike. Twice I'm asked for money; one moves his hand down the back of his jeans. A knife, an itch: I don't wait to ask; I run.

I see a hotel — Hotel Reforma — as shite as a hotel can be. I head for it. In the foyer is a waterless fountain; a Christmas tree, somehow wilted even though it's plastic. The room is a film set for a suicide. A lightbulb blinks sallow light on a sagging mattress, a 2009 calendar hangs. Television bolted down; toilet roll holder padlocked. Through papier-mache walls: voices, music, horns, dogs, and the dull thud of a football being kicked — at one point, a hellish scream. Anything, though, at this time, will do. If all they had free was a dog basket in the backyard, I'd say, "Looks great; which corner do I crap in?"

ANTIGUA

"*Marcos, que tal?*" says Maria Elena, the Guatemalan woman I've moved in with. She runs a homestay in Antigua, renting rooms empty now that her sons have left home. I've been here a week, trying to learn Spanish. Three times a day we sit at the dining table under a mothballed lampshade, a stack of warm tortillas before us, and engage in conversation that for me is like trying to crack a safe. My Spanish still sucks, but I've found some hacks: Words that are the same in both languages — *final*, *ideal*, *normal*. And words that are the same but with an *o* or an *a* at the end — *problema*, *fantastico*. And being creative with the basic words that I know: *Manana* means tomorrow, so for the day after tomorrow I say, "*Manana, Manana*." Every morning we discuss what we're doing that day. I've been to church, baked cakes, cycled for miles: so she thinks, anyway. I'm an athlete, in her mind, a dedicated Catholic. Not someone who spends their days snoozing and listening to podcasts. Today she says something about three dead brothers. An odd thing to say at breakfast. *Her brothers? How did they die? All at the same time?* Questions I would ask if this conversation were in English. As it's not — and I don't know the vocabulary to ask those questions, and may have anyway misunderstood what she said — I sidestep the issue by pretending I didn't hear, and say that today I'm climbing a volcano.

Which is true. Voluptuous volcanoes — Agua, Fuego, and Acatenango — surround Antigua. Slumbering Acatenango, which last erupted in 1972, overlooks its simmering sister Fuego and is the third highest summit in Central America. That's the one I'll climb. The tour agency warned me that it's a cold, hard slog and that several tourists died of exposure on Acatenango almost a year ago to the day. I nodded solemnly, then pointed at my Chelsea boots and asked, "But I can wear these, right?"

"No," he said. "No, no, no."

That I'd worn them into a silver mine held no sway. He insisted; it was a deal-breaker. I'd need at least trainers, ideally hiking boots.

So I go to the market to see what I can get for cheap, thinking for a couple of quetzales I'll get a pair of once-worn Nikes. But at the three second-hand stalls I visit, there's only one pair in my size: Mizunos that appear to have once been owned by a marathon runner. Though picked from the garbage, the guy wants £12 for them. For that price, surely I can get new ones. Fifteen minutes later I'm sat on a stool surrounded by mounds of trainers rejected for being *pequeno* — too small. I'm only size nine, but I'm made to feel like a freak. Some have stopped shopping to stare at me. It's as if I'm a Brobdingnagian shoe shopping in Lilliput. The salesgirl at last finds a pair in size nine but they're luminous yellow. A hike isn't a catwalk, but I have standards. I end up with a pair of hiking boots. Made, I suspect, by a syndrome in a sweatshop. The tag and logo say they're Timberland, but if they're Timberland, I'm Ranulph Fiennes. They only need to last, though, until tomorrow: afterwards I'll give them to a homeless person.

Fifteen others are with me for the trek: Swiss, Dutch, French, German, Japanese, Costa Rican, Peruvian, Brazilian. Six are gum-chewing, oh-my-God American college girls. I'm the sole British representative and feeling the weight of expectation that comes with it. Some of history's greatest adventurers have been British: Dr. David Livingstone, Robert Falcon Scott, Ben Fogle. On the bus ride to the volcano we make a stop to sort out unprepared people with items of kit. A sorry choice of jackets hangs in a line on the wall of a shed. It's first come, first served. I'm not one of the first. I choose a black jacket, not for its warmth but for its colour, which matches my jeans and boots. Back on the bus, a Swiss woman asks, "Why did you choose a women's jacket?"

"Is it?" I say. "How do you know?"

"The buttons; they're on the left side."

"I thought that was a Guatemalan thing."

"And look at the shape of it; it fans out towards the bottom."

I look down. She's right.

We set off on a path of soft, ashy soil, following the head-guide Gilmer. It's steep from the outset, a torturous trudge. The first break comes after fifteen minutes — and it's needed. One of the American All-Stars has already given up. After an hour, the struggle sets in for all. Sweat drips from faces strained and suffering. It's not the distance or the incline, though both are factors, but the altitude. It makes the air thin, reducing the oxygen intake on each breath. Being young and healthy is no defence; the fittest of the fit can suffer altitude sickness. A friend told me that taking Viagra helps. I didn't. I feared it was a joke, that he thought it would be funny if I had to climb a volcano with an erection. And it would be funny if it were someone else. So I'll pass on that advice to others.

The group splinters. I'm in the lead pack, one of half a dozen. Not that it's a race. Unless I'm first to the top, in which case it is. Some slowed by backpacks too heavy; they've packed as if they're going to live up here. I only packed snacks and water — three litres, the minimum suggested. A Dutch bloke carries his bird's water as well as his own, and a dozen bottles of Gatorade and a store full of snacks that he dispenses on her demand like he's a vending machine.

I tell him, "There's no chance I'd carry three litres of water up here for someone."

"Not even your girlfriend?"

"No."

"If you love her, you have to."

"One litre — if she were my wife and we'd been married at least twenty years."

Talking uses up limited breath, but conversation is a distraction from the struggle. To pass some time, the Brazilian asks me to teach him some English swear words. I oblige: "... bloody ... fucking ... dickhead ..."

An All-Star passes, shakes her head. "Whatever he's done," she says, "he doesn't deserve to be called that."

Up, up, up we walk; steep and twisting through thickening greenery until we're in dense woods. The dirt path is now muddy gravel; every so often there are stairs, almost vertical, made from packed mud and tree branches. Then into alpine forest. On breaks the chill is felt. On one we pose for a group photo. Most have borrowed a jacket; we look like the window display for a charity shop.

At a stop on an outcrop I see Antigua nestled below. It's the beauty to the beast that is Guatemala City. A lattice of cobbled streets of colonial buildings in a citrusy palette, ornamented with terracotta and stucco. A green plaza skirted by the stately facades of Catedral de Santiago and Palacio de los Capitanes Generales. Cafes selling over-priced cappuccinos. It could have been so different: Guatemala City is the abomination that Antigua would have become. A seismic catastrophe conversely saved the city. Reduced to rubble by a 1773 quake, what was one of the New World's finest cities was all but abandoned. It lost its capital status to Guatemala City. Antigua became "the old city", bypassed by progress; resurrected centuries later by coffee and tourism.

We walk on, ever higher, piercing clouds; then onto a flat path, crunch of gravel under foot, and work our way around the volcano until a sight to behold brings us to a halt: Fuego. Barren slopes, black as ash. A column of smoke from its cone. It raises spirits; the pace picks up. Then a boom like a crack of thunder. Sparks of molten shoot into the sky and red-hot rocks skitter down its sides. All are wide-eyed in awe, transfixed by nature at its rawest, the guts of the earth thrusting from core to crust to cloud.

After five hours we reach base camp: a row of tents and a

pile of firewood on a ledge that looks out to Fuego venting its fiery fury. One of the All-Stars arrives an hour after everyone else, hauled along by one of the guides. "Oh my God," says one of the others, rising from a lie down to run over and hug her. "We were so, so worried about you."

Not that worried, I think: they left her behind three hours ago.

"What's the wifi password?" I ask one of the guides as a joke.

"Oh my God, they have wifi?" says an All-Star, excitedly reaching for her phone.

We look at her, waiting for the smile.

"Well, what is it?" she asks, serious.

No wifi and no toilets.

"Number one?" says Gilmer when I ask where to go.

"Yeah."

"Anywhere."

I unzip my flies.

"Anywhere but here!"

I walk ten metres away, do my business there. Men, let me tell you: If you've never had your todger out on a volcano, it makes a man feel like a man. Even if at the time you're wearing a ladies coat.

As the light slips from the sky, Fuego slowly slides into silhouette, then disappears into the darkness. Nightfall magnifies its magnificence. The brooding monster rumbles and growls. Violently it hiccups, streaking lava bombs through the air. All the fireworks you've ever seen set off as one. A memory forever.

A fire is lit; on logs that circle it we sit; our faces flicker in the burn of the blaze. In a pot greased with butter, spaghetti cooks over the fire. Gilmer spoons portions to people. Their tired eyes say, *Please, sir, can I have some more?* I skip my share. Pissing al fresco is fine; shitting is uncouth. A spliff is passed. Slugs of rum from a bottle shared. Talk of where we've been and where we're going, the lowlights and highlights of the big wide world. And ruminations on the fragility of this strange planet we call home: a wafer of crust on a flaming mass of rock. And what we are: parasitic squatters, expendable. As the fire fades, I'm one of a few that remain under a bed of stars bright and bountiful. I can sleep any night; only tonight can I watch a spewing volcano. In total, a couple of dozen eruptions.

At 4am: *Zziiipppp.* "Time to go to the summit for sunrise," says Gilmer, smiling. I'm not smiling. I slept for only thirty minutes. Not because we had a slumber party, up all night pillow fighting and playing spin the bottle — which, with the All-Stars, I'd have been keen on — but because of the cold, the altitude, the adrenaline. We step out into the pitch black. *We* not being everyone: two are ill and three aren't allowed due to being too slow. The final climb to the summit is 400 metres. Doesn't sound a long way: the 400-metre world record is 43 seconds. But Wayde van Niekerk didn't set the world record on a 60-degree slope of volcanic scree and ash. With a plastic bag on his head. At 4am.

A death march begins, a Frodo-like ascent to Mordor. Every step is the energy of twelve. All turns to grey: jeans and jacket, hands and face. I'm ashen as a week-old corpse. My lungs also feel grey, as if for breakfast I've smoked twenty fags. I focus not on the unseen summit, only on the next step: *One, two, one, two, one, two.* No time for small talk, only grunts and swears. "Ugh, argh, bastard," I mutter. The lanky German in front turns to look at me. "Not you, mate," I tell him. "I'm talking to the volcano."

A verging on vertical incline comes next, as punishing as anything I've ever encountered — at a time when a walk in the park would be painful. On all-fours I scramble. Hands pick up the slack for feet that flag. I kick in toes to get a grip, grasp with fingers for a handhold. To slip, to misstep, is a tumble that will end in more than tears: flesh ripped by rough scree, bones broken by boulders. My head throbs, my heart hammers, my lungs heave, my vision blurs. I'm on the brink, being forced into submission. I'm not alone in my struggle. Some are unsteady, stood swaying; some are crouched and heaving, or sprawled on the ground — a guide goes to one and tells him to turn back, that to go on is to risk his life.

I steady my breathing, breathe through my nose. *Breathe deep, breathe slow, deep and slow.* Then I push on. And progress I make until I crumple onto my knees. "I'm done. I can't go on." My body is on strike. My spirit is broken.

"Come on, man," says the Costa Rican. "It's only one more minute."

I lift my head from my hands, hope in my eyes. "Only one? I might be able to do one more, if that's all it is."

"One more; maybe not even that."

He helps me to my feet. I stagger onwards.

A minute comes and goes, the peak still not in sight. "Where's that Costa Rican?" I say to the beanpole.

"He's gone on ahead."

"I need to catch up with the liar so I can slap him. And thank him for getting me going again."

At last a levelling: a desolate plateau. Nothing green, nothing alive. On the rim of the bleak crater, people wrapped in foil blankets wrinkled by the thrash of the wind. Shivering, sipping from thermoses. Tired faces force smiles for selfies. Nods of respect exchanged. Only ninety minutes, but it feels as though we've spent a week at war. Dreams of Everest ended: I used to think, *It can't be that hard; people with no legs have been up there.* But a wreck scaling a minor peak, I concede I've no chance.

The reward for the struggle is a spectacle unrivalled: a sky suffused with a spectrum of orange and pink; a final fire in the hole from the Devil's chimney.

"*Fantastico,*" I say to the Brazilian, stood beside me.

He nods slowly, smiles, says, "Motherfucker beautiful."

LAKE YOJOA

I'm in the woods, squatting in the bushes, equipment in hand, patiently waiting. The bird I want is black and big-breasted. I'm not fussy, though. Anything will do. I'll take a cock. I can hear them, chirping melodically, chorusing their conversations. But it's difficult to pinpoint the location; even to tell what's a bird and what's not. I track down one that looks almost like a flower. Focused in with the binoculars I borrowed, I realise it is a flower. Over an hour I spot a few: the Red-legged Honeycreeper, the Violet Sabrewing, the Gartered Trogon. And that will do. I'm only birding — here in the Cerro Azul Meambar National Park — to make myself appear cultured, so I can say at dinner parties, "Oh, you just have to go birding in Honduras; fabulous, my dear, wonderful." Dogging, on the other hand, is a different matter. Mention dogging, you'll be lucky to still be there for dessert.

Birds seen, I follow a path into cloud forest pristine and primeval, canopy so thick it mutes the light. I pass waterfalls and cross flimsy wooden bridges, springy under foot. I inhale earthy odours, listen to the whispers of the forest. At one point an outcrop: a picturesque panorama of the forest and the hills, and Lake Yojoa, the largest lake in Honduras. Often I fear for the world, fear it's being destroyed by a plague of people, disfigured beyond repair with our concrete, our pollution. Then I see a sight like this, or the Copper Canyon in Mexico, or the highlands of Guatemala, and think, *It's not too late, the end is not yet nigh.*

A walk alone in the woods is such a joy. Until it's not. Soon it's a slog, and the path that was gravel degrades to soggy mud. Seduced, though, by the scenery, I push onwards and upwards, deeper and deeper into the forest. The slippery ground slurps, my footsteps squish and plop. The mud becomes ankle-deep and so thick it acts like glue, pulling off my flip-flops. Could I?

Don't be silly.

But then maybe just this once?

Get a grip of yourself.

But I think I'll have to . . .

Like a modern Mowgli — barefoot and muddy, but wearing skinny jeans and with an iPod — I ease my foot into the mud. *Ooo, that's kind of nice.* Liberating to be barefoot on nature's carpet. If no footwear feels this good, perhaps I should strip more off. Nude could be orgasmic. But if I'm starkers except for binoculars, can I still claim I'm birding? Only the most liberal of judges would believe so. Barefoot makes me more nimble; not like a ballet dancer exactly, but more so than normal. It's as if feet evolved for this purpose. Barefoot, though, won't go mainstream. There's no money to be made from it, so the suits won't let it happen. It's beyond even Bezos to sell people their own feet.

I start to adapt in other ways: I crouch slightly for a lower centre of gravity — this helps but gives my gait the look of an ape — and after cleaning my dirtied hands on damp moss I browse the forest like it's a supermarket: that twig would make a useable toothbrush, that leaf I could origami into underpants. I duck under fallen trunks, clamber over others. I grip vines for support, push off rocks for momentum, and inch across high, stony ledges slick with sodden leaves. My inner commando — not seen since Beavers — soars in confidence. *Maybe I'll stay here*, I think, *live a pure life, at one with nature.*

But that's fantasy to think I could be a 21st-century Tarzan. Truth is I'd be shivering in the bushes, eating slugs.

I return to Los Naranjos in the undeveloped heartland of Honduras, where coffee grows, cacao too. A nothing-town with no ATM, but next to Lake Yojoa. Forest borders its shore on all sides. The water, edged by murky marshes, is windswept and black as night. Later I'm out on the lake in a two-man kayak with Slavi — a Croat with a head the shape and shine of a cue ball. I swore I'd never again go kayaking after disgracing myself on one a few years ago. I said no this time, but was persuaded. It would be a leisurely venture, they said, with stops for beers and fried fish. They lied, I say, soaked through, blisters on my hands, the only buildings dots in the distance. The Bulgarians we set off with — the persuaders — are motoring like they're running on batteries, methodically machine-like. Slavi and I are in feeble pursuit, behind by a hundred metres. Our moans and groans and grunts pierce the quiet. The Bulgarians probably think we're so far behind because we've taken a break to have it off with each other. Besides the Bulgarians, we're alone out here. Not a boat nor a kayak in sight.

After three hours Slavi and I stumble out the kayak and kiss the grass like we've crossed the Atlantic and have discovered the Americas. The building we guessed to be a restaurant, the only reason we came all this way, may as well have been a mirage. It's post-apocalyptic: long-ago abandoned and boarded-up. Cans and bottles on the ground, shrivelled inflatables in the empty pool. We leave the kayaks, clamber over a fence and cross an overgrown football pitch, its goalposts broken. We pass a pair of kids on a rusted seesaw, who stare, point, whisper. A dirt road leads from the forest to the shore; strung along it are a few dozen rustic homes in states of disrepair. No supermarket, no restaurant, no bus stop, no taxis.

A muscly bloke sawing a plank looks up; he stops sawing, pulls up the rear of his baggy jeans. We start to stutter our babyish Spanish when he interrupts, speaking with a redneck drawl: "What you guys doing here in Las Marias?"

We explain our situation; ask where we can buy food, how we can return to Los Naranjos.

He says, "We don't get many tourists come here now. You're the first in a long, long time. Ain't no reason to come no more. They used to come on boats. No one came on a kayak before."

He puts down the saw, wipes his hands on his vest. "You can't buy nothing, but you can come to my house to drink coffee, and I can ask around, see if someone will give you a ride."

We follow him — his name is Juan — into a shell of a one-storey house, humble as a home can be. No doors, no glass in the windows — not even walls inside, just frames where they should be. An artificial Christmas tree lays on its side in a corner; a dog sleeps in another. In the back yard, a woman turns the wheel of a mangle-type machine, grinding beans; a rooster struts about her. A boy holds a rabbit, gently strokes its ears; his brother beside him plays with a drill. Juan lists the names of those who live in the house; it's a long list for a house with only one bedroom — which doesn't yet have a bed.

We sit on plastic chairs, nibbling biscuits and sipping coffee. Juan — who's fifty-three but could pass as forty — picks up a guitar and plays *La Bamba* for us, then a medley of songs about God and Jesus. He says after that he lived in Georgia for twenty years until he was deported; then he returned to Las Marias, where he was born.

"I've done some very, very bad things," he says, his beatific smile fading for a second as he stares off into space. "Really terrible things, you know."

I'd like to know, but feel it's rude to ask.

His grin returns. "But now Jesus Christ has touched my heart. He's changed my life, man; now everything is good, good, good. He forgave me, so I can forget those things and go to Heaven."

I ask, "How long have you been a Christian?"

"A couple of months."

Our ride comes, so we go outside, leaving some money on the table. Unasked for, but surely welcome. People with almost nothing, sharing the little they have with people they don't know, won't meet again. They treated foreigners as friends.

The ride is a battered pickup truck, the price £20. We'd have paid £200 — anything to avoid a return by kayak. Had they charged me my soul, requested I submit it to the Lord, I'd have agreed, would have handed it over right after retrieving it from the Devil, who I pawned it to in 1996. We load the kayaks and oars into the back of the truck, having to angle the kayaks — which are each as long as the truck — upwards over the cabin to fit them in, making them look like missiles. Slavi and I wrap ropes around the kayaks to try and keep them in place and tie knots that would shame a scout. The Bulgarians sit up front, Slavi and I in the back — me under the kayaks, among some trash. "God bless," calls Juan, waving as we drive through the village, almost obliterating overhead power cables. We ride along a rough, windy road. I slide about, my head bashing the kayaks. One slips off the cabin, is angled off the side of the truck, positioned like a lance. Oncoming vehicles swerve out our way, decline to joust with us. We only stop to reposition and retie the kayak when a man waves us down to hitch a ride.

After half an hour we arrive in Los Naranjos at the house we hired the kayaks from, heads hung in shame. Anyone who sets off on water but returns by road has had a mare. The man we rented the kayaks from runs up from the lake, where he's been looking for us, worried we've sunk. Or, more likely, worried his kayaks have sunk. No one goes kayaking for five hours. No one wearing jeans, anyway. "Las Marias?" he says, surprise evident, when he asks where we've been. "So far."

I'm staying at D&D Brewery, a place that doubles up as a

hostel and a microbrewery. Cabins in the woods, chairs around a firepit. Hummingbirds zipping from tree to tree; pussies in bushes, eyes alert and darting. In a shed is a pub: hundreds of banknotes pinned to its walls, scrawled with names of past patrons; a row of shiny draft taps: Porter Cafetero, Pena Blanca, Meambar, to name a few — brewed on-site in a shipping container, the inside of which looks like a meth lab. On stools lined at the bar, a gathering of guys from Peru, France, America; snacking and chatting, playing backgammon. Numbers exchanged, friend requests issued. We all know we'll never meet again, but that's a detail for later. Right now we're brothers bonded by beer. A corporate lawyer chats to a bloke cycling from Belize to Costa Rica. A Belgian brags about cows and beers and breasts being better in Belgium than anywhere. A local drinking to destruction after the death of his father is slipped a valium to soothe his despair. Ernesto — another deported from the US — serves the drinks. He says, "I have thirty-two brothers." Everyone laughs, but he insists he has. It's true, confirms another worker — but it's thirty-two brothers and sisters, not just brothers. Ernesto says he hasn't met all of them. "We're spread across Honduras and America. Maybe one day, I hope." A family portrait, I joke, would be an artist's lifework. And his family tree more like a family forest.

Some of the talk is of politics; not Trump or Brexit, but the Honduran variety, which sounds like it's scripted for Hollywood. At last month's election, with over half the vote counted, the current president, Juan Orlando Hernandez, was trailing the opposition candidate — Salvador Nasralla — by 5%. Then, for thirty-six hours, counting stopped.

When counting restarted, Nasralla's advantage steadily eroded, and Hernandez had the lead by the end of the count, winning by 1.5%. The independent Organization of American States investigated and said there were irregularities, that for Nasralla to lose from the position he was in was statistically improbable. But the result stood — and was backed by the US, who favour the right-leaning Hernandez.

Hernandez shouldn't even have been on the ballot. The Honduran Supreme Court lifted the constitution's prohibition of presidential re-elections — a measure to safeguard a country cursed with a history of crooked statesmen. The five judges who made the decision owed their positions to Hernandez. People were pissed about that, and also other things: Food prices have risen, as have taxes; and resources have been flogged overseas with the proceeds pocketed by politicians.

Enough was enough: After the election charade, riots ripped through Honduras. But were violently suppressed. Dozens died.

Hernandez is to be sworn in for his second reign next week at a ceremony in the capital Tegucigalpa. Opposing parties, though, have called for chaos to cripple the country, to continue until they get a rerun of the election: A strike and roadblocks, a shutdown of airports and borders. Revolution is on the cards. Hondurans have the firepower for it and a taste for blood: gun-related deaths per capita are one of the world's highest, 500% higher than the US.

Tourism has already bombed, says Ernesto, since the trouble after the election. Those at D&D Brewery are leaving the country pronto, exiting before the chaos ignites. But not me. I'll go to Tegucigalpa.

TEGUCIGALPA

The day of the presidential inauguration. The day a sash is placed on Juan Orlando Hernandez, spelling the start of four more years of power. All but a few tourists have high-tailed it out of Honduras. Only the mad and the stupid remain.

I head downtown, on the way asking a man for directions. He says he's going that way, that I can walk with him. I tell him I'm English not American. I've said that to every local I've met on this trip — at the outset, so they're clear. Hondurans — and Mexicans and Guatemalans — have lots of reasons to think Yanks are dicks, none to think Brits are. Not that I know of — but, I'll admit, I don't know all that much.

"Big Ben. Sherlock Holmes," the man says, when I tell him I'm from England.

"And the Queen," I say.

He doesn't understand.

"*La reina*," I say, translating.

"Ah, girl king."

I ask what he thinks about Hernandez.

"*Presidente es un . . . ,*" he says.

The last word I don't understand, but get its meaning. One of the short, sharp words in a language, spat rather than spoken.

He asks what I think of Honduras.

I tell him, "*Honduras es bueno.*" Everywhere is *good* when a local asks me. I save my stones, cast them on the page.

Plenty to throw at gritty, greyified Tegucigalpa. A corpse of a city, as shite a capital as I've seen: tired, sagging, depressed. Hotchpotch bare-bones buildings, stripped naked, half beaten, starved. A few — those of the wealthy — are built like bank vaults, burglar-proof and also seemingly artillery-proof. High walls and barbed wire and barred windows. Alsatians and armed guards. Hills ring the city; their slanting, charmless neighbourhoods are off-limits to outsiders, under the rule of gangs. Atop one is a large statue of Jesus.

No anarchy but a sense that it's simmering. Sirens wail, low-flying choppers circle. Freshly-sprayed graffiti: *Dictator, Corrupte, Fuera JOH*. Soldiers and police stand in twos and threes on corners. Larger groups in trucks, as though massing for battle; bright eyes peeled through jet-black balaclavas.

The man and I cross a littered canal, climb some steps, turn a corner. A block ahead, a three-thick barricade of uniforms geared for a riot: shields, batons, guns. Frontline fodder, the pawns of the politicians.

"*Seguro?*" I ask the man, wanting to know if it's safe to be here.

He makes a balancing gesture with his hand: fifty-fifty.

Security forces aside, downtown is business as usual. Shopping, snacking, chatting. So much for the strike, the protest, the revolution. The main square, Central Parque, is bordered by dreary, dull-toned seventies buildings. Off it leads a high street of lowlights, of peeling, decrepit shopfronts. Brand names on sale are secondhand — "*Ropa Americana. Todos 50L*" — in stores akin to jumble sales. It feels like some town up north — Bradford or Doncaster or Rotherham — you've heard of but never want to visit. Not much of a prize to be fighting over. Like children squabbling over a sandcastle as the tide comes in.

I hang about a while to see if anything happens. I think, *If there's no revolution by lunchtime, I'll go back to bed.*

Half an hour later on the high street, a smattering of civilians start to jog. A ripple of concern spreads, upping the pace of more. I join some in standing on tiptoes to peer down the street, trying to see the cause. A mob of red ahead, bound for the square. Masks, scarves, balaclavas. As I retreat to the square, I move through the gears: jog to run to sprint. As I go, on either side, doors lock and shutters slam.

I stand at the far side of the square, next to a bandstand; on benches beside, black-handed shoeshiners shine shoes. The mob pour in and surround a statue of a man on a horse. Horns blare, firecrackers explode. Wooden machetes jabbed at the air, "Fuera JOH" painted on the blades; and white crosses, on each a name, city, age — details of people killed during the protests. Some have flags draped over their shoulders; others wave flags in the air. Two scale the statue, tie flags to the top. The flags are red and say "*Libre*" — the name of the coalition against Hernandez. I look to the armed forces; they stay in place beside a shuttered McDonald's, blocking the street to Congreso Nacional. Visors down; batons raised; shields braced. They don't intervene, but they do reinforce. They number several hundred.

A convoy of cars arrives in the square. Out steps Stetson-wearing Manuel Zelaya: orchestrator of the coalition and a former president — ousted in a 2009 coup by Hernandez and his allies. With Zelaya is Salvador Nasralla — Hernandez's adversary on the ballot paper. His hair dyed, his face botoxed. He's famous for being a television presenter, has no political experience. The crowd cheers their arrival. Bystanders begin to clap. A pickup loaded with speakers pounds a cheery song on repeat; the crowd sings along, hands in the air. Zelaya schmoozes. Bright white teeth beam under his bushy black moustache. The two then stand on the statue base, take turns to shout speeches. "*Revolucion,*" is the keyword, repeated.

The crowd swells but considering the stakes is small. A fly on a bull. I've seen more people protest the opening of a new Tesco. One of the most dangerous countries in the world, and for a revolution they rustle up a thousand people for karaoke. If 1% of the population swarmed the square — nearly a hundred thousand people — that would be a statement. The world would watch.

Hondurans, though, have been intimidated into inaction. Dozens killed during previous protests. Hundreds wounded, detained. Activists and journalists especially targeted: threatened and harassed; imprisoned, beaten, shot. It's one thing to side with the protests in private, quite another in this climate to do so publicly. But you can't ask for a revolution. Sacrifice is required.

Zelaya and Nasralla blather for half an hour then fizzle without climax. A lull sets in. An ice-cream vendor pushes a trolley, rings a bell. A few buy one. Outrage is undermined, in my opinion, if you're licking a Cornetto. I move closer, sit on the steps of the cathedral. I think: *What this needs is a spark, a few angry, young tearaways, protest pacesetters to bull-doze the boundaries.*

A minute later it happens.

I look to the left: soldiers suddenly steadying their feet, stiffening their shoulders. I look to the right: a spearhead of protestors has broken from the rest. Arms pull back, rocks in hand. Cries of war as the primitive projectiles are cata-pulted. I'm up quick, fleeing as a hail of rocks thuds shields. That was the catalyst; retaliation is coming. Over my shoulder I see a gap open in the line; a man steps into it, his eye to the lens of his gun, the butt pressed to his shoulder. *Bang.* Pause. *Bang.* Canisters fizz forward, land and crack with a flash. Whiteness engulfs the square. Pandemonium.

Downtown becomes a battleground. Gas and stones traded in scrappy skirmishes. Shouts echo, car and shop alarms sound. A newsstand on its side, a street sign uprooted. Bystanders hunched and retching, red eyes streaming. An ambulance screams down one street; a dirt bike takes to the sidewalk to overtake a jammed queue of taxis. Men in crash helmets spring from a UNE TV truck, microphones and cameras in hand. The revolution will be televised. In side streets, the military square-off with ragtag knots of wild-eyed hooligan-like protesters. They wear red shirts and hard hats, dust masks or scarves; or are topless with their t-shirts wrapped niqab-like around their faces. "*Puta*," they yell, arms aloft and out wide. Gas is shot at them, suffuses the streets like fog. Canisters are kicked to touch as soon as they land; I see one scooped by a gloved hand and returned first-class to sender. Rocks rain down, a dozen at a time. Most the size of bricks. Or actual bricks. One group fires while a second reloads. They look for cracks through which to flood into the square. Tentatively towards the enemy; two steps forward, one step back. Ground gained, though, they lose just as soon. The military robot-like, strategically synchronised and systematically splintering defiance with tactics drilled, drilled, drilled. *Bang.* Pause. *Bang.* Then through billowing whiteness the stomp of three dozen black boots, a row of perspex shields — printed on them: "*Policia Militiar*". The shifting nature of the fight turns safe spots to frontline in seconds. Gas feels like acid in my throat, tastes like the smell of fireworks. I turn one corner to see soldiers bearing down, a few metres away. *What am I doing with my life?* I wonder as I run. I'm at risk, could take refuge at the hostel. This, though, is history. So I stay. But with a safety strategy: from a bakery I buy a cheese pastie. I'm not hungry, but with it I'm less likely to be a target. A stone's thrown, they'll look for the perpetrator and think, *It's not him: he's eating a pastie.*

I take a break at a cafe called Paradiso. Arty-types drown their sorrows while singing along to rock. There I meet a bloke called Warwick, who's staying at the same hostel. He's an Aussie freelance journalist; tall and wiry, ruddy-nosed, white-haired. He drank beer for breakfast while Skyping his mother. "Ma, stop fucking panting down the phone," he shouted at one point. I order a Coke, Warwick a beer and tequila slammer.

Warwick and I hitch a ride in the back of a pickup to the

national stadium, to try and get into the inauguration ceremony. But we're too late. Outside the shabby bowl, trash is collected and the streets are being hosed. To avoid a flashpoint, the time and place were secret. Stadium at 3pm was the rumour. Location correct but the time — 9am — wrong. A few hundred attended. Invite only. The main protest, I find out, was this morning a couple of kilometres from the stadium, as close as barricades permitted people to get. Thousands protested. Until gassed, dispersed. They split into smaller groups; one headed downtown and was what I came across earlier.

A taxi returns Warwick and I to downtown, drops us by the congress building, behind enemy lines. A couple of hundred police: black body armour, visored helmets. All have batons; some have guns, canisters strapped to their chest. I start walking backwards; Warwick forwards, in among them. He pulls his camera from his gilet, asks the leading officer if he can film. The officer assents. With his camera, and due to his age, Warwick looks like a pro; me, not so much. I stand beside him, no obvious purpose. If I weren't so slight, they might think I'm his bodyguard. As it is, they probably think I'm his boyfriend.

Back at the square, the ground fiercely fought for is now free. But though order is restored, reminders that not long ago unrest unravelled: broken bricks and burnt-out tyres, a carpet of glass outside Burger King — its windows shattered. Expended canisters litter the floor. I pick one up; in blue print on the metallic casing: "GL-203/T. TRIPLE TEAR GAS CHARGE. Do not use after expiration date." On another: "MP-43-CS. CS SMOKE PROJECTILE. SHORT RANGE. Use only outdoors. Do not fire directly at persons."

Warwick speaks to locals, records interviews. Until there's a bang and raised voices, a commotion on a side street. Twenty rough-type red-shirts, coughing and spluttering, jog into the square. A minute later one of them grabs a fist-sized piece of rubble, adopts the pose of a javelin thrower and starts towards the police lined by McDonald's. His gift is air-mailed. I flinch in anticipation of a bang that doesn't come. Gas, no; men, yes. Batons thump against shields as they march in formation across the square. Warwick doesn't back up even a step — being pissed steadies your nerves. Stone sober, I skitter like a spooked horse. One of a posse of dolled-up prostitutes shouts at the leading officer: "I fuck your brother-in-law." One of the others, a transsexual: "And I fuck your brother." The police demand the whereabouts of the rock-thrower; they're pointed in several directions. They split into groups, head off.

Sporadic fighting later, but the battle, it's clear, is lost. The war too. Democracy died today in Honduras. Killed by dictatorship.

ESTELI

I'm staying at Iguanas Hostal, a single-storey sketchy kind of place in Esteli, a city on the Pan-American Highway in the north of Nicaragua near the border with Honduras. My room is large, spartan, abysmal: stained sheets, stray hairs on the pillow; toothpaste left by the sink, a sim card on the floor; mismatched furniture, splintered and chipped; a window missing half its glass slats. But a bed is a bed when you're tired, and it was a full day of travel from Tegucigalpa — only 230 km, but four buses, two taxis, two walks.

I slept alright, ate breakfast at a nearby cafe, washed some shirts in the sink in my room. Now I'm looking for places to hang them to dry. *What's that?* I think when I see white powder smudged onto the small desk in the corner. *Sugar? Salt?* Dab and taste. Tastes like cocaine. Dab and sniff. Definitely cocaine. Under the desktop is a drawer. I open it, see a snowdrift. I pull out a lump as large as a Werther's Original. I roll it between finger and thumb, thinking. A chocolate on your pillow, a towel in the shape of a swan: these are things you might expect to find in your hotel room. A drawer of cocaine, not so common. Santa didn't bring me it: Christmas was a month ago and I've been naughty in more ways than one.

Jackpot! I at first think. Anxiety, though, creeps in. I could dine on this stash for a month, but if I'm caught with it I'll be dining on jail meals for a decade. I'll be one of those scallywags seen on those low-budget Channel Five documentaries — "Steve, from Liverpool, was imprisoned at Al Wathba in 2011 after he was caught at Abu Dhabi airport with seven kilograms of heroin stuck up his anus."

My room opens onto an inner courtyard — withered shrubs and doors to half a dozen guest rooms. No one is about except a blonde-haired German, sat at a table eating cereal in the centre of the courtyard. I tell him what I found.

"How much?" he says.

"A shitload." I show him a photo.

He says, "What are you going to do?"

"I don't know."

He puts down his spoon, says, "We could . . ."

"Could what?"

"Take some."

"I thought about that. Do you . . ."

I trail off as I recall entering Nicaragua yesterday at the Las Manos border crossing. As my mind replays the scene, a chill drills down my spine. The four-eyed, gel-haired penpusher at the immigration building — a shipping container repurposed — was an arse. I stood in drizzle talking through a perspex window. What's usually a formality — a minute, more or less — was thirty minutes of suspicious questioning. *Profession. Single or married. Where and when I started my trip. Where and when I'll finish. The route I've taken thus far and will take from here. The places I'll go in Nicaragua. Where I'll stay in Esteli. The address of the hotel. How many nights I'll be there.* I hadn't booked a hotel but had details of one noted in case I needed an address to give a taxi; I told Four Eyes that was where I'd check in. Four Eyes recorded my answers — on a piece of paper, not a computer. At one point he disappeared for fifteen minutes with my passport and the paper; when he came back he asked how much money I had on me and how much I had in the bank. I told him. He left again. On his return, he let me enter the country. I was asked no questions when I entered Guatemala and Honduras. And at no border I've ever crossed — dozens of them — have I ever been asked how much cash I have on me and the amount I have in the bank. Yesterday I thought little of it. I thought: It's a jobsworth doing his job. Now, though, I'm concerned: I'm asked how much money I have and what hotel I'm staying at, and then a shipment of cocaine appears in my hotel room. Coincidence? Or the cocaine was planted for a sting, and the police will soon swoop?

Or maybe it's nothing to do with the feds, but with the locals in the room across from mine — the only other guests. A couple of forty-something Clipart crooks, off their faces last night. One had a motor mouth grinding between gerbil cheeks, a belly bursting through a check shirt, a cap he kept taking off only to put back on. The other had equine features and sallow skin, wore one-size-too-large clothes that sagged on his wasting frame. They were drinking in the courtyard, jabbering as coke fiends tend to. When they entered or exited their room it was with a furtive glance and a sideways squeeze through a marginally opened door. Both were in my room at one point. When I arrived, there was no lock on my door; it was busted clean off, just a hole where it should have been — another strand adding to my paranoia. But I was told not to worry, that one would be fitted; a couple of hours later it was. Before it was, though, I was laid on my bed, swatting mosquitos as I listened to *The Totally Football Show*, when Horse Face strode in and paced in circles, muttering to himself. Then he went in the bathroom, came out with a tissue, and wiped several surfaces. Weird, but he was drunk, and drunks can be weird. He might, I thought, even be the owner, feeling guilty about the state the room was in. While he was doing that, Gerbil Chops came in and ranted about his wife of twenty-three years leaving him last week because she heard him on the phone to another woman. He claimed innocence. After the rant he tried to persuade me to go with him to a whorehouse.

And then, this morning, another strange thing. When I left for breakfast, in the courtyard I encountered Horse Face and a trampy terrier of a woman chavved-up with bling and tracksuit bottoms. Her face, pudgy and round, topped with short, black curly hair, looked like a testicle. Horse Face and her both had the fried-eyes expression of people up all night. She was savage, shouting. He was trying to calm her, stop her from leaving. When she saw me, she ran to me. The dilated pupils of her unblinking eyes were an inch from my face. She rabbited incoherently — part Spanish, part English. I thought she said "police" and "drugs" in the tirade, but it was so jumbled I wrote it off as garbage. "*Loco*," the receptionist whispered to me and twirled her finger by the side of her head. At one point the terrier held her hands up with her wrists crossed; at the time it meant nothing, but I now recognise it as a gesture of being handcuffed.

So: The cops? The crooks? Collusion of some kind — the cops made the crooks plant the coke so the cops could later bust me? Or a coincidence?

"Don't take any," I say to the German, and give a brief rundown of what happened at immigration. He was in the courtyard yesterday evening, politely putting up with an earful of nonsense from Gerbil Chops and Horse Face, so knows for himself about that pair.

I look for the receptionist so I can find out what she knows about it. But she's not here. I walk laps of the court-yard; stand up, sit down, stand up, sit down; drum my fingers, stroke my chin. An idea: move the desk out of the room. When I try to move it, though, I find it's stuck to the wall. If I can't move the coke out of the room, *I'll* move out of the room — distance myself from the mother lode. I grab my stuff, throw it down by the table in the courtyard.

She's still a no-show after half an hour. I start to ques-tion whether I even want to find her: she might phone the police, and I don't want that. I wonder: *Maybe I should knock the door of the Mad Hatters, ask if it's theirs?* No. If it is, and they know that I now know it's there, they might think I'll tell the police, and take action to keep me quiet. *A runner?* Yes. I'm too close to that Sahara of cocaine. If the police come — either because it's a set-up or because of those lunatics — being in the courtyard instead of in my room won't help: that pile of powder is being pinned on me. My fingerprints are all over the scene and in the toilet is a log of DNA evidence that won't flush.

My bag hastily packed, I return to the room. If I might

have to do the time, I may as well do at least some of the crime. *Snniiiffff*.

The German, infected with my paranoia, is in his room packing. I tell him I'm off.

"Wait for me," he says.

"Sorry, man, got to go."

"Just a—"

"Bye."

Except I can't go: A corridor connects the courtyard to the street, and there's a gate between the corridor and the courtyard, and the gate's locked. Full-blown panic sets in: *It's a set-up; I'm being framed.* I shake the gate, try and fail to wrench it off its hinges.

The girl, I remember, the daughter of the receptionist; she had keys in her hand last night, and she's about somewhere: I saw her when I returned from breakfast. "*Llave?*" I ask, when I find her, sat on a sofa in a back room. She doesn't understand. I know that's the word for *key*, but I can't pronounce it properly. I say it again and again and again, trying different pronunciations.

"*Llave?*" she at last says.

"*Si, llave.*"

"*Si, tengo.*"

She skips off; skips back with a set of keys. We go to the gate; she unlocks it to let me out, then locks it again. The door to the street, though, is also locked. I turn to see the German at the gate, the girl unlocking it for him. This one too, I tell her, pointing at the front door: "*Rapido.*" Her tiny hands fumble with the lock. The German and I are like horses barred in at the start line of a race. It opens, and we bolt — the German one way, me the other.

Now what? Go to the police? Hope that coming forward proves my innocence? But they might smell money and stitch me up. Or want me to give evidence against Horse Face and Gerbil Chops, hang about for weeks to go to court. Screw that. Their witness protection program is probably a stick-on moustache. *Another hotel here?* No. They — the cons, the police, whoever — might hunt me. There are few hotels in Esteli; it wouldn't take them long. *Hide in a bush until it blows over?* That could be a week, a month. If I spend that long in a bush, I'll turn feral. *Get out of town?* Seems sensible. To the bus station. A bus to anywhere but here.

At the station, a beat-up yellow school bus about to leave has "Matagalpa" painted above its windscreen. Where that is, I don't know, but it will do. I board and take a seat. I fidget, avoid eye contact. In the window I catch my reflection: a sweaty, sketchy bloke stares back at me, nostrils flecked white. *How the fuck*, I think, *did this happen?* An hour ago I was chilling in a cafe, drinking coffee, eating eggs on toast, wondering whether to tinker with my fantasy football formation — 4-4-2 to 4-5-1? Now, it's not yet 9am, and I'm charged up like Scarface, on the run from a ten-stretch.

MATAGALPA TO LITTLE
CORN ISLAND

I holed up in Matagalpa for a few days. I stayed at the hill-side Hotel El Castillo, a place crudely modelled like a castle. I got a room with a balcony so that I could make an Escobar-like rooftops escape if the federales swooped. Several times I searched Google News for "cocaina Esteli" to check my photo didn't show up. I read about corruption and prisons in Nicaragua and fell down a Jason-Puracal-shaped rabbit hole. Arrested for drug trafficking, American Puracal was imprisoned for nine months before the case made it to trial. At trial he was convicted, sentenced to twenty-two years. A year later, under pressure from the US Government, he was granted an appeal. His conviction was overturned. He spent those near-two years at La Modelo, a maximum security facility where he was kept in a tiny cell with a dozen others. His hair fell out. His gums bled. He lost 15 kg. After I read about Puracal, I nearly went to the airport: escape while I still can. But if my card is marked, there would be no escape on a 747. I'd be handing myself in, and looking guilty while I did it. I may as well run free for now, face up to reality a week from now, maybe a year. So I've opted for a cross-country journey to the Caribbean, tempted by Little Corn Island into a diversion from Rio de Janeiro. For what could be my final days as a free man, I'll swim in the sea, eat some lobster, impregnate a local — so someone will feel obliged to visit me in jail.

At San Benito, 100 km from Matagalpa, I have to change buses. Three full ones come and go. People board, but I refuse to be one of those tossers that gets on a bus that's too busy. I wait in a cafe; its TV plays music videos: women wearing little, shaking boobs and butts. A nun clad in black stares at the screen as she noshes. Noticing the inappropriateness of the channel choice, the owner changes it to the news. The news is gruesome footage of bullet-ridden bodies. Two more bursting buses later I board one that's packed. (I am a tosser.) Skin rubs skin and sweaty odours radiate, permeate nostrils too close to the source. I sit on the dirty ledge where those sat on the back row put their feet, and slowly stuff cold, salty fries into my mouth. Curtains patterned with flying geese drawn across the windows, and on a fold-down screen Van Damme rampages through Shanghai, noisily battering Chinamen. A vendor pitches packets of magic beans, spiels that they'll heal this, cure that; he shows an album of rank before photos and miracle after ones. All sorts of crap no one wants is sold on buses in Central America. A shopping channel that can't be changed. In time I get a seat — at least part of one. A buttock and thigh spill onto my seat. Arses on buses should be like carry-on luggage on planes: "Sorry, madam," the driver should say, "your rear is five inches too large; you can't come on board with it. Please see my colleague over there, who will fit you in the hold." No respite from the aisle side: the bloke there has no regard for the position of his pecker; he pounds me with it like I'm some kind of wank sock. I stare at the drawn curtain, recount the geese: *One, two, three ... twenty-seven ... one-hundred and eighteen ...* This is the shitcake of travelling. You can have the cream and cherries, but only if you swallow a slice of the brown stuff. If you turn up your nose at the taste, you're done before you start. A bakery's worth I've eaten: It's the price to be paid, and I'll pay it. Because taxing as any trip can be, the trauma is soon forgotten. Afterwards thirteen hours become a passing thought, condensed into a second. And having suffered the torments of travel, how sweet those cream and cherries. So I say with a smile: "Supersize, please."

Once Big Bum leaves I take the window seat and open the curtain, watch pitiful place after pitiful place pass by. Unfortunates employed in wretched labours. Streets befouled and trash-strewn. Clumsy, shambly buildings — "Live Today" mocks a tagline painted on one wall, an advert for junk food. Nondescript nothing-towns to the traveller; potholes on the road to paradise, places they only come so they can go. Yet everywhere has characters and scandals and secrets. Where there are people, there are stories. Sometimes I think I'll jump off at such a place, stay for a month, maybe a year. Arrive a stranger, leave as the mayor. I did in fact live a year in a minor place — Dan Chang in Thailand. To a person passing through, it had neither attraction nor merit. An archetypal nothing-town. I taught at the school and side-gigged at the hospital (teaching not operating). I played football with the locals, ate at the restaurants, drank at the bars. It was one of my best years. Good as it was, I was glad to leave. I could get off the wheel, escape the cage. To be born there, though, is to be trapped. I remember one girl, a former student of mine: she was in all the top sets, a hard-working-bookish-type. Of my 500-plus students, she was one I'd banked on to hit some heights. Returning for a visit a couple of years after I left, I saw her — then nineteen — grilling kebabs at the market. "What's that girl doing here?" I asked my ex-boss. "Didn't she go to university?"

"No," said my ex-boss. "She has to stay here to help her mum with the family business."

"What family business?" I asked. "You mean this kebab stall?"

"Yes."

Born into a dead-end, she had no chance.

After a few hours a change of scenery: green, grassy, wooded. Through the kilometres the landscape thickens and darkens, the rivers widen and brown. No towns now, nor hardly a village; instead a peasant society, raw, rural living, simple abodes spread sparsely. Arms filled with fire-wood, donkeys heavy with sacks; pigs feed on gutter scraps, vultures circle, scout. "*Se Vende Esta Finca,*" a sign states, spray-painted on plywood. "This Farm Is For Sale." The farm is a hut and a pair of cows. Hiding there I would be hard to find. A new life off the grid, just me and the cows. One for milk, one for a wife.

The bus ride ends at El Rama. Tedious drizzle has

turned the town into a mud pit. Tuk-tuks and buses fleck brown the faces of those traipsing in the quagmire. El Rama is the end of the line; the only road out is the one in. From here to the coast, in fact all of the province of Atlantico Sur — 20% of the country — is a region where there are no roads. Onto a boat next to ride the Rio Escondido to the Caribbean. I board a *panga*, a type of elongated speedboat, floating on the murky river, and wait for it to fill — that being the time to depart rather than the time stated on the schedule.

On the boat is John, a Canadian in his sixties. He sits with limbs splayed; a toned chest shows through his undone shirt. Between puffs on cigarettes he monologues a catalogue of bullshit and boasts. "My sister bred the best horses in the States," he says. "She created a US-German hybrid breed that won gold across the board in show jumping at the Olympics. A Spanish prince bought one of her stallions for a million bucks. She liked me to stay with her and help with the horses because I could talk to them."

"Talk to the horses?" I say.

"I could do that after learning to talk to whales."

"What? Whales?"

"A guy I knew, a very smart person, asked me to help with a project he was working on at the time, learning how to speak to whales. I'd spent a lot of time at sea, rigging equipment, and he needed an expert diver to set up his specialist equipment underwater so he could send sonar signals to the whales and record the signals they sent back. It took a while, but it worked: we could speak to the whales. He should have won a Nobel Prize for what he did, but of course he didn't because he wasn't Jewish."

I tell him, "Lots of non-Jewish people have won a Nobel Prize."

"Name one."

"Barack Obama."

"Obama? He never won one."

"He did. A few years ago."

"How did he win one, after the millions of Africans he killed?"

"Africans? You mean Arabs?"

"No, Africans. The US is always running experiments in Africa — secret ones, obviously — trialling untested medicines and biological weapons. They've killed millions, believe me."

I see my reflection in his mirrored Aviators: I look like I don't believe him.

"Anyway," he continues, "Obama is Jewish. He was born in Kenya. Africa is the original homeland of the Hebrews."

"His Dad was Kenyan, but he was born in the US to a US mother."

"That's what they want you to think, the Government. But I've seen photos of his mother arriving on a plane from Kenya. She flew into not just any airport, but Washington DC. That's proof. No arguing with that."

I realise that's a lost cause, so I start back on the whales: "What were you talking to whales about?"

"Anything we wanted."

"Basketball? The weather? Where's the common ground?"

"Well, one thing, we could tell a whale which way to turn, and it would turn that way."

"That's fifty-fifty. It has to turn either right or left. I could shout at a whale to turn left, and half the time it would."

"We talked about more than that — lots of stuff."

"This guy, his findings were published? Approved by his peers?"

"The project was cut short before his work could be completed. At the time, no one knew why. Then — after I'd lost contact with him for years — I randomly bumped into him at Heathrow. I knew he wasn't right when we were chatting, then an announcement came over the tannoy and he ran off saying the son of Christ was calling. I thought it then, and someone else confirmed it later, that what had happened was the pharma companies drugged him to make him go mad."

"Why would they do that?"

"He was on to something, that's why. You see, this equipment he had didn't only let him talk to whales; he could communicate with any animal. I saw him do it, getting foxes and all sorts to come up to him."

"Why would pharmaceutical companies care about that?"

"Because as well as talking to animals, he found that it was attracting organisms invisible to the eye, that could heal the body and mind. No way the pharmas could allow that to happen and put them out of business."

"Maybe he just went crazy on his own. Talking to foxes is kind of mad."

"Definitely the pharmas that did it. They interfere in anything that puts their profits at risk. I work here in Nicaragua for a doctor who specialises in stem cells, injecting people with them to cure all sorts of problems.

The pharmas have lobbied to get it banned in most countries. Nicaragua is one of only a few places you can get the treatment."

"You've tried these stem cell injections?"

"I sure have. I had one last year, and at sixty-five I'm in the best shape of my life."

To be fair, he's in good shape for a sixty-five-year-old that chain-smokes. The doctor, though, should have prioritised another operation: stitching his lips.

When twenty people have squeezed onto the boat, the rear engines gear up, and we're off. We start sedately before switching on the afterburners, slicing a furrow through the water, leaving a spray in our wake. We swerve driftwood, take waves like speed bumps. Long-legged houses shaded by palms, and rusted trawlers half-submerged, whiz past in a blur. A Bond-style getaway. My exit from Esteli on a yellow school bus was more like Bean.

We zoom into Bluefields, a penurious coastal city. A white church set among colourful buildings deliciously dilapidated, their facades faded by the sun, worn by storms. Shadowy drinking dens and bowls of fish freshly gutted, dingy alleys and creaky jetties. I board the once-a-week ferry bound for Big Corn Island. Lucky ones are indoors watching *The Mask*; the rest of us outside: sitting on benches that face off the side or sitting on the floor. Men load goods and produce, slot it around passengers in space that should be for arms and legs. A police officer boards, beelines for me. Bollocks: I had to show my passport when I bought the ticket. "*Pasaporte,*" she demands. I hand it over. My body tenses, my heart pounds. She looks at the ID page, then at me; does this a few times. She twice thumbs through the pages, saying nothing, then returns to comparing me to the photo. She hands it back. She goes to another foreigner; then another, and another. She checks everyone's. I need to chill: I'll be fine until I reach the border. The Nicaraguan police aren't the FBI. I bet their national criminal database is a Rolodex.

A rough and tumble voyage ensues, the not-so-sweet Caribbean swirling violent swells. Showered in sea, we're soon soaked through. The cheeks of the woman beside bulge. She swallows. Bulge again, then swallow. Her head moves from her hands to through the railings. She spews over the side. She slinks to the floor, sprawls with eyes closed. Her son strokes her head. More spews come from her and others, streams of the stuff. John, who said he spent years at sea working on ships, is one of those vomiting their souls. This boat and the series of buses before is a journey for the hardcore. A flight from the capital Managua to Big Corn Island is only £70. The boat is £6 and the buses a quid or two. But that £60 saving is a bonus, not the reason. The point of travel is to travel, and a plane isn't so much travel as primitive teleportation. By plane you see almost nothing of a country. To see it, to feel it, ride buses the length of that country, take trains, take boats, even walk. That's the way to know a country: travelling through the hinterland, the hard-pressed, pants-down provinces; pondering the people in their natural habitat, putting yourself in their shoes — seeing if they even have any. Those strange names on a map — seen in person, if only for a minute, if only through a window — confess more than any capital, any beach or church or museum, are more truthful than any guidebook.

We dock at Big Corn Island, 70 km off the mainland. Big

Corn Island — 10 km², 6000 people — would be fine if there were no Little Corn Island a half-hour panga ride away. Little Corn Island — 3 km², 1000 people — has no roads and no cars, no banks and no ATMs. From 6am to 2pm, there isn't even electricity.

LITTLE CORN ISLAND

"Sorry," a woman says to me.

I'm sat on the beach; she's just come over: what does she have to be sorry about? Maybe I misheard. "What?" I say.

"Sorry."

"What are you sorry about?"

"No, you sorry."

"I haven't done anything."

"Not sorry." She makes a jabbing gesture with her finger, motions at my clothes with her other hand. "*Negro*. Sorry."

Negro, in Spanish, means black. I say, "Zorro?"

"Yes. You Zorro."

She walks off, laughing.

I stand out on this palmy white beach, where bodies in itsy bitsy teeny weeny bikinis bronze in the sun. I'm the only one in jeans and a shirt. The only one in black. But it's not like I've come in a burqa, as some of the staring suggests. A situation not helped, I suppose, by being on myself. To be a man alone on a beach is stressful — even if you're not dressed for a funeral. People think you've come to perv. A split second of eye contact is classed as leering; for all they know it's been half an hour. And if you've any smear of suntan lotion on your hands . . . If they're topless, it makes it worse. To try to explain is only to dig deeper: "I wasn't looking, honest, but from what I saw when I wasn't looking, they looked . . . erm . . . nice. Nothing I haven't seen before, of course. I mean, not yours; I haven't seen yours before. This is the first time — not that I'm keeping a record. I've seen plenty of . . . erm . . . mammary glands in general. Not plenty, just a normal amount. On TV, online. Not that I go online to look. Sometimes it just pops up, out of my control. I mean, a window will pop-up . . ." Face down in the sand is safest. Prepare before is the other option. Come at dawn and lay two towels, say your girlfriend is in the toilet. "She's been a long time," a curious person may ask after an hour. "Dodgy shrimp salad last night," you say with a grimace. Never a follow-up question after that. Or build sandcastles and pretend you've come with a child: "The little tinker sometimes goes missing for days at a time; don't worry about him." Whatever the strategy, it's a lot of work to avoid being weird.

After a few hours I tire of being the freak, and have offended too many to stay — "What are you staring at, Ms Bombatty? Sitting in your shadow, that half of the beach think the sun has set." — so I cross the grassy headland at the end of Otto Beach and trace south along the eastern coastline: tiny coves and empty virgin beaches, bays the shape of horseshoes, settings for stories of castaways, stretches of solitude where you can spend an hour and see no one. Passable as paradise, albeit a rugged version.

Beaches stained with plastic and polystyrene, tangles of gunk-topped browned seaweed. Sullied too by eroded shorelines and gnarled mangroves, a blackened swamp and beached trawlers. Homes also are ragged: small and squat, rusting rooftops and windows without glass, clumsily cobbled together with a mishmash of materials. Some are sturdy, have second storeys, are colourful — can even be called fancy. Fewer of those, though, than there are corrugated shanties. It feels as though they're marooned, making do with Lord-of-the-Flies-like temporary measures while they await rescue.

Boys scout for coconuts: one prods a palm tree with a pole-vault-length utensil; another tries his luck with a catapult. Men chop and shovel; women with babies watch them. They sing and whistle and listen to reggaeton on decades-old speakers. One lobs grain at chickens over a barbed-wire fence, its posts made from branches on which panties hang to dry. One hands a husk to a white-faced monkey tied by the neck to a stump. Most prefer to snooze. Their skin is as dark as the sky is blue. On necks and wrists gleams bling. Board shorts they wear, with baggy t-shirts or vests that bear the names and logos of American sports teams and colleges. Little is new, lots of holes. More in common with their cousins in the Caribbean than their Nicaraguan brothers. Including language: they speak a spiced English with such a lilt as to be largely unintelligible, like listening to a radio with the signal scrambled. So strong and stereotypical is the accent that I question if it's an affectation: "I know it's silly," a teacher will say to her class, "but tourists love this shit, so we have to keep it up. Now, all repeat after me, 'Wagwaan'?'"

"Ya, boy," says a man with a gilded smile, as he holds out his fist to me.

"Aiii," I reply, as I bump it with mine. "Respek. Wassup bredren?"

A blank look. He walks off.

Another — a Caribbean Bill Crosby — mimes toking a spliff and says, "Ju wan some ganja, mon?"

"No, thanks."

"Wat 'bout da white den, eh?" he says, and pretends to sniff a line. "Gud stuff dis, man, gud, gud stuff."

Circumstances being as they are, there's not a chance I'll buy, but I ask about the price for reference purposes. You know you're in Latin America when you think £15 a gram is a rip-off.

A dirt path leads me to "downtown": a slender wooden jetty, a string of coloured buildings spread along a simple concrete sidewalk: Little Corn's superhighway that stretches for a portion of the west side of the island. Fishes and flowers engraved in the cement; at one point a hopscotch. Someone has written "Happy". It's walked by people bare-foot, people pushing wooden handcarts and wheelbar-rows. Some carry planks on their shoulders or sacks on their backs, lemming-like as they stream in single file. A few speed demons bicycle — mostly blokes on kids bikes. A small cargo boat is unloaded, a once-a-week delivery. Other boats bob about offshore: New Future, Eagle One, Thunder: a few of the names painted onto their aged sides — apter would be The Past, Ostrich, Fart. Worn-out lobster pots smoulder to white ash beside nautical paraphernalia, and buckets overspill with the day's catch. Banana pastries and coconut bread sold at stalls, a slender selection of groceries from gran-run stores. A cafe-bar advertises, "Tonight: Sabu (The Catman), all the way from Bluefields," and on the sand a Rasta-themed restaurant: The Shack; Marley hangs on its walls, the menu says, "Breakfast served until 5pm." A few hippies, some Yoga nerds. Spliffs and guitars, coconuts spiked with Flor de Caña. Comatose is the ambience. It feels as if it's off-season idleness, but this is in fact the season.

I walk to the thin south of drumstick-shaped Little Corn, taking one of the loose, rough trails through the jungly forest that covers almost the whole island. Sparse and secluded, for fifteen minutes I don't see a house nor a person. By now I've gone native and am barefoot. Twigs and stones under foot, I move as if I'm trying to introduce a trendy dance all the way from Bluefields. When the path peters out to nowhere, I take to rambling through thicket and scrub. I reach a clifftop, see fifty metres away, on a rocky headland, a naked woman. She must have thought herself safe way out here, beyond a trail to nothing. She sees me; there's an awkward moment. I slope off, think to myself, *That's a kind of lesson about life, about sticking to the path even when it seems to be taking you nowhere, because naked ladies await those who persist.* A few minutes afterwards, while trying to shortcut a return to the path, I come out closer to the woman. Except it's not a woman; it's a man with long hair. Another lesson, this one more practical: time for an eye-test.

I return to my *cabana* at Elsa's on the windswept eastern shore. I sit in a crudely-crafted wooden chair out front the yellow beach shack that looks like a wendy house DIYed by an alcoholic father. It's shite, but £10 is a bargain for beachfront accommodation. Clusters of cabanas like this are spread around the island, as well as stilted huts with palm-frond roofs, priced up to £40 per night. Prices for rooms and food are double that on the mainland, but you can get by on £20 a day. That such a place at such prices still exists is difficult to believe. It has its inconvenient location — far from the Pacific-side hotspots: San Juan del Sur, Ometepe, Granada — to thank for being unspoilt. It can't last; money will wake it. Now there's a single five-star resort (£200 per night); a decade from now, surely more. Foreigners have already begun to set up, seduced by the stress-free utopia where happy souls live slow lives in the sun. The two main cafe-bars in the village are foreign-owned, and walking around I saw plots for sale — "4SALE ½ Acre. Totalal@msn.com" — and also pricey properties: "Custom House on ¼ Acre. $175,000. See House At littlecornrealestate.com." Seeing those I added a new No.1 to my desert island survival strategy checklist, downgrading "Find a water source" to No.2: "Make a sign: 'Welcome to Markland. Plots 4SALE 4 £99,999.99'".

Perfect place to visit, but live here? Sun and sand, beers and boobs: unbeatable, some say; that it's how they plan to spend their retirement. But bumming on a beach, getting drunk and high, is a dream not a plan. A month or two of that and you're bored. So small is this island that it would be like living in a sand globe. Same buildings, same people, same paths: day after day after day. I saw the same woman today at several places; at what point does it become stalking? Eight? Nine? Should I already be on a watchlist? And paradise is only paradise until you live here. Chores are chores; aches are aches; bills are bills. Same shit, different destination. It's the human condition to complain, to find fault. You're bitten by bugs, the wifi sucks, it rains . . .

It rains now. I take refuge inside, as outside a storm rages. Wind whistles through the skew-whiff woodwork. The roof rattles and leaks drip. I shower under a trickle of chilly water, wonder about the inch-wide holes in the walls: better to give than to receive, says the Bible; Jerusalem, though, didn't have glory-holes. No mirror — fine: how many hours we would save in a world without mirrors. Also no wifi — a break from baby photos: everyone thinks theirs is the Second Coming despite the statistical probability that by the time it's twenty-three it'll be an office chimp. So under the feeble light of a naked bulb, beneath the hole-ridden mosquito netting that cloaks the sagging mattress, I lay and listen to the rhythmic rattle of the rain, and the roar and rush-back of the tide, nothing to distract me from the terrifying thought that tomorrow I'm thirty-five. The average life expectancy for men is seventy-nine. Thirty-five rounds up to forty, and forty is nearer to seventy-nine than zero. I'm more or less dead.

EL CASTILLO

"THE COURAGE DO NOT DEPEND ON SEX: A GIRL THAT STOPPED THE ADVANCE OF A GREAT EMPIRE," says the seemingly Google-translated headline of a display within the Castillo de la Inmaculada Concepcion — a castle stood grand on a hill in the centre of El Castillo, beside the fast-flowing Rio San Juan, in south-east Nicaragua. "In 1762 the British forces besieged El Castillo, where took place the heroic exploit of Rafaela Herrera, a girl who barely was 19 years old. The young lady Herrera, educated in manly exercises and expert of the manage of the weapons, took herself the boot-fire and shot the first gunshots, with such happy success, that the third killed the English Commander. At nightfall Rafaela ordered to soak some sheets with alcohol and to throw them out to the river on floating branches. The current dragged the pyres towards the enemies' boats that frightened to see that Greek fire decided to retreat."

She was the daughter of the commander who had died

the week before, and with a hundred-or-so compatriots repelled an attack of two thousand.

The castle isn't large, but it's brawny and cleverly situated at a sharp bend of the river at a point where are perilous rapids: ships would have to slow, making them easier to shoot. Spaniards built it in the late 1600s to fend off the pirates of the Caribbean, who sailed the 200-kilometre Rio San Juan from the Caribbean Sea to Lake Nicaragua to plunder the interior of the country, particularly the honeypot of lakeside Granada, one of the jewels in Spain's empire. Impenetrable was the fortress until the arrival in 1780 of an Englishman with a cunning plan. That man was not Baldrick but Nelson — yes, *that* Nelson. His plan: anchor the battleships at the coast and take a couple of hundred soldiers in rowboats upriver towards the castle; then, out of sight and range, take to land through the dense jungle and spring a sneak attack from a hill at the rear of the castle, and lay siege until the dastardly Spaniards surrendered — which they did. But it was all in vain: decimated by disease and distracted by other missions, the British never made it to Granada to implement their strategy of seizing the city to slice in half Spanish America.

The top of the castle is a place to propose marriage, the panorama perfection: rainforest fringing banana groves; the river, wide and brown, snaking into the distance; the remote village of El Castillo, tranquil and colourful and cute-sized: 1,500 people — small enough to know everyone, large enough to not have to marry a relative. No roads to it: the river the way in, the way out. Between here and the coast, 100 km away: nothing. San Carlos is the nearest settlement, 40 km upriver. Rickety wooden buildings stand on stilts along El Castillo's riverbank, where is a path lined with cheap cafes and low-key lodgings and living rooms set up as stores. Cacao beans dry on sheets spread on the ground, plump pods grow on trees in yards. A man cycles with fish hung off his handlebars. Muddy wellies tramp to and from fields. To offset the sedateness, a women's softball match. A crowd cheers from a shacky stand and sows and cocks wander the outfield. American-style baseball kits, complete with masks and mitts. Underarm pitches, looping, straying no-balls — one after the other, again and again. At last the crack of bat on ball; it flies over the inept leap of a fielder, who falls over on landing, narrowly missing a cow. The batter sets off; her arms flap as she goes. A home run: she slides in at fourth base just as the ball, via three fielders, returns.

The Rio San Juan forms the southern border of the Indio Maiz Biological Reserve, 3,000 km² of rainforest. In it resides a wealth of wildlife: armadillos to jaguars to agouti to pumas. And downriver from El Castillo: hundreds of crocodiles. I set off to see them with a girl named Karen and a couple of French retirees, Cecil and Jack. Eduin is our guide, the local Rambo and Romeo, an El Castillo native returned after a career as a semi-pro waterskier. He wears board shorts, a white vest, a camo hat. A machete in a leather sheath hangs from his waist. In a kind of motorised gondola we putter along the turbid river, swerving branches and trunks. To the left is the rainforest; to the right Costa Rica. The river the border between the neighbours. No fence, no border patrol. A man could easily slip in unnoticed. A man worried, for example, about a drawer of cocaine. The rim of the boat is a mere 30 cm from the water;

Jack rests his arm on it, his elbow off the side. Sat behind, I reach forward and clamp my finger and thumb on his elbow. A retiree has never moved so fast. A string of French expletives as he flails and thrashes to escape the jaws of the croc. The French, it seems, don't have the same sense of humour as the British.

A spotter, sat on the bow of the boat, scours the banks for signs of life. "Look," he says.

"Look where?" I say. "At what?"

He says, "An iguana in that tree."

"What colour is the iguana?"

"Green."

"This tree?"

"No, that tree."

"There?"

"No, there."

"This one?"

"Not that one; this one."

"That one?"

"No. There, that one."

A green iguana in a green tree in a jungle of green trees: the world's hardest magic eye.

Further on is a mid-river island with cows on it. I ask Eduin, "Who put those cows there?"

"No one," he says. "They swam there."

"Cows can't swim."

"They can."

"The size of their body, the size of their legs: I'm sure they can't."

He's sure they can.

If cows can swim, pigs can fly. Anything's possible.

We come to a military checkpoint — a few sheds painted in camouflage — where we stop to check into the reserve. A Nicaraguan flag hangs limply and soldiers stand smoking with assault rifles slung over shoulders. One, who's fishing, is wearing a Bob Marley t-shirt; on the front is an image of Bob in a cloud of smoke, holding a joint. Paperwork is checked; the boat is searched. Eduin says, "Last week some guys were caught with four kilos of coke." I expect a story about them being caught in the depths of the jungle, perhaps spotted by a helicopter. "They were on a bus," he says, "riding out of San Carlos."

I ask why they would risk a bus when they could travel unnoticed through the rainforest.

He says, "They'd probably be killed by a puma or a snake or something. And it would take them weeks. On the bus it takes only six hours." He says a friend of his was arrested on a bus going north to the capital Managua. "He did it for four years before he was caught."

Further downriver, hundreds of white egrets gather in the reeds, and a spindly lizard runs on its hind legs across the water, past a turtle sunning itself on a rock, and a spider monkey meanders across treetops, it's long tail used as an extra limb. And there, beside a small island dense with stalks of bamboo, the rusted boiler of a wrecked steamboat. A steamboat — an American one — out in the wilds of Nicaragua isn't as odd as it seems: this river helped connect the Atlantic and the Pacific before the birth of the Panama Canal. In the mid-1800s, fortune hunters from as far afield as New York traversed this route to reach California, where the gold rush had hit. Ships entered the Rio San Juan from the Caribbean and sailed across Lake Nicaragua; then passengers transferred to stagecoach for a short land leg to the Pacific to take a second ship. It was faster and safer than to travel by land across America. The journey, though, was rough. "Many people complained," it said on a display at the castle, "that three times a day they were served crackers and rotten pig."

We turn down a stream, one of many that stretch for miles into the mass of green. The motor is cut and paddles are taken to hand. We then alight for a 3-km hike. The trail, Aquas Frescas, is one of only two. The rest of the rainforest is off-limits to all but the military and the indigenous Rama and Kriol people. A sort of static plays — noise but imprecise — and it's so humid that I feel as though I'm wearing a woollen wetsuit in a sauna. Slowly and sweatily we squelch through shin-high quagmire, through smothering undergrowth. Creepers swaddle trunks thick with thorns, and jelly-bean-sized alien-like insects swarm over moss-clad branches on which grows fungi of a dozen types and hues. Sloths are about somewhere, lounging in the canopy. Slow as they are, they should be simple to spot, but we're struggling. It's only 2pm; they might, I suggest, still be in bed. Howler monkeys are an easy find. A bunch are roused by our presence. The alpha roars. Eduin says that if howler monkeys think you're intruding on their territory, they throw shit at you to warn you off. If they do that to me, I'll launch a dirty bomb of my own.

"Poison frog," says Eduin, dropping to his knees and poking about in the foliage. "They're tiny, but blue or red, which makes them easy to see." Back on his feet — the frog got away — he says, "The tribes that live here, they used to rub the points of their arrows on the backs of the frogs;

that's where the poison is, to prevent other animals eating them."

I ask, "Animals the tribesmen shot with the arrows would die?"

"It didn't kill them, just made them weak and dizzy for a couple of minutes, which was enough time to catch them and kill them with a knife."

I ask what would happen if a person were shot with one.

"It would do the same as it does to animals, make them weak and dizzy. I've felt the effects when I've held the frogs in my hands to show people. If your hands are sweaty, the poison seeps through the pores of your skin."

As we trudge through the barbarous landscape, "Don't touch anything," warns Eduin repeatedly, like we're toddlers in a china shop. Snakes are a worry, their shape and colour such that they're meant to blend. The venomous fer-de-lance resides in these parts: one of the most deadly snakes in the world.

Eduin says he's killed a lot of snakes; I ask him how to do it.

He says, "Beat it with a stick to knock it out, then cut off its head." The stick is needed for keeping it at a distance. With a knife alone, even a machete, by the time you're close enough to slash you'll be bitten. "It'll be so quick you won't even see it strike."

Eduin shows us a photo of paw prints in mud. "This was a couple of days ago on this trail. A Jaguar." I'm not scared: I'm not faster than a jaguar, but I don't have to be; I only have to be faster than Cecil and Jack. But Eduin says no one need worry. "They run away from people; they don't like the smell."

Pumas are less fussy: Eduin says last year, not that far from here, one mauled someone. He says someone else was eaten by wild boars. "They left nothing of him. No bones, not even his hair."

"Then how do you know wild boars ate him?" I ask.

"He told friends he was going out to hunt a wild boar, and where they found his rifle it was clear from the scene what had happened. The ground was trampled, and a tree had been knocked down that had on the trunk the marks of wild boar tusks. They're vicious and move in groups of as many as a hundred. If you go after one, you risk all of them coming after you. The guess is: he shot at one, climbed a tree when the whole group came at him, and they took down the tree then ate him. Even his boots were eaten. Only his rifle was left."

Deforestation suddenly sounds a grand idea. Let's drain the rivers too, make the world as safe as we can.

Down another stream we pull over on a silt bank. Sunlight strobes through the canopy into the creek — a scene from *The Jungle Book*. While Eduin cooks chicken and vegetables, and the others sit on a log and chat, I take a walk on my own. How long, I wonder, would I survive on myself in this savage place? Because I'm nothing to nature. It gives not a crap more about me than it does a bug. A night: I'd back myself. A few days: yeah. A week: maybe, but I wouldn't bet on it. I can't run, so I'd hide. I'd dig a hole large enough for me to fit in, and cover it with leaves. Eduin says when he stays in the jungle he lives off ants and nuts and fish, but I wouldn't chance roaming around for lunch when I'm on the menu for others. I'd eat in that hole, shit in that hole, sleep in that hole. The piece of gum in my pocket would at a push last a day. Fingernails would sustain me a few more days. Toenails for the rest of the week. Then I'd start on my fingers, left-hand pinkie first. I stop walking, stand atop a boulder by the stream. All is still, but I sense that things unseen see me. A pile of stones is to my side; my hand poised to pick and throw. Weapons are mankind's advantage, even the simple stone. With stones I'll defend my territory. Defend it to the death. Or until I run off. Because if tools are man's edge, our ruin is our fear. Frightened of spiders, afraid of mice. Some are scared of balloons. We are pitiful. Me as much as anyone: I flee when I see a spine in the stream. (I say spine, it may be a twig. By the time I'd be close enough to be sure, I'd be close enough for it to be too late.)

Back on the Rio San Juan, on a clearing on the riverbank, posed like a statue, a crocodile. It turns its icy gaze on the boat. A second later it slopes into the water. Its eyes and spine remain visible for a second longer, heading right at us, then it submerges. It doesn't reappear. More come: a croc on a rock, one on a sandbar. We see several over half a dozen kilometres. Each time it's, "Argh, a bloody crocodile." No one sees a croc and says, "Aww." Steve Irwin faked his love for them to pay the bills. It's the mouth, those hellish gnashers. The body of a croc with the mouth of a frog would scare no one.

"American crocodiles," Eduin answers to me asking what type they are. They grow up to six metres, live as long as eighty years. Saltwater, freshwater, swimming pools: as long as it's wet they can live in it.

I ask what they eat.

He says, "They eat whatever's nearest. Fish, mainly, but

also birds, sloths, and monkeys, if they come down to the river. Cows too."

I make a note: *If I ever have to swim in croc-infested waters, to halve my odds of being eaten, swim with a cow.*

He says he knows of four attacks on people along this river in the last ten years. Three died.

I ask what to do if faced with a crocodile.

"In the water, you have no chance. It will drag you down, then spin you until you drown."

"But on land there's a chance?"

"Run if you can. But don't turn your back on it if it's within a few metres. They're quick over that distance."

"And if you can't run?"

"They're slow to turn, so circle around the back of it and jump on it, then clamp its mouth closed with your hands."

"You'd need to be pretty strong to hold its mouth closed."

"Closing its mouth, it's strong and fast; opening its mouth, though, it has a lot less strength."

"So you're on its back, clamping its mouth with your hands; then what?"

"Wait."

"For what?"

"Help to come."

"That could be hours."

"Then you wait for hours."

"If you get tired, let go?"

"Then you're fucked."

MATINA DE LIMON

The minivan crosses a bridge over the Rio San Juan to reach the Las Tabillas border crossing between Nicaragua and Costa Rica. Panic eased as the days went by but has again flared. None of the many I've spoken with were quizzed like I was on entering Nicaragua — and no one else found a drawer of cocaine in their hotel room. At the end of the bridge we pull over by a marquee. A border officer enters the van to inspect IDs and passports. I'm the only Westerner. She flicks through my passport, notes down my details on her clipboard, and hands it back. I'm keen to drive on to Costa Rica before those details are entered into a computer. But a couple are taken to have their paperwork double-checked and their bags rifled through. And when they come back, a man goes to take a pee. If I knew how to say it in Spanish, I'd say, "Mate, piss your pants. I'll buy you new boxers and jeans in Costa Rica, and slip you a hundred cordobas for your trouble." When he returns from the bushes we drive for a few minutes then all alight at a barrier across the road. The flag of Costa Rica flies ahead, fifty metres away. But I'm not yet in the clear: a hut is beside the barrier, and the man within wants to see my passport. He also has a clipboard instead of a computer. He's more like a car park attendant than someone protecting a border. He thumbs through my passport, then waves me past.

I'm safe.

At the Costa Rican immigration building I hand the officer my passport. He asks where I've been in Nicaragua. Strange: *Why does he care about that?* I look at his uniform; the badge says "*Nicaraguan Micracion*". The bloody *Inception* of borders this is: a border within a border within a border. And this bloke has a computer. He scans my passport, stares at the screen a while. He calls over a colleague. They browse my passport, then call over another colleague. I'm again asked where I've been in Nicaragua. Discussions between them. Minutes tick by.

It turns out it's not *that*. The issue is me not having an entry stamp in my passport. *An oversight? Part of the plot?* They decide they don't care and stamp me out.

I'll never know the truth of the matter, whether it was the cops or the crooks or a coincidence. Maybe I was saved from above. To keep my karma in credit, I'll dedicate my life to saving those less fortunate than myself. When I say life, I mean week. When I say those less fortunate, I mean sea turtles.

The Refugio de Vida Silvestre Laguna Urpiano is on Costa Rica's eastern coastline. The nearest town to the refuge, Matina de Limon, isn't much of one; from there the refuge it's twenty minutes by taxi, ten more by boat. At the refuge I meet Barbara, a biologist from Spain, and

Johnny, her Costa Rican partner; and a couple of live-in workers — Gerardo and Maximo — and three volunteers, German twenty-year-olds. Four years ago Barbara and Johnny started the project from scratch. It's still a work in progress: the boat I took here was loaded with planks of wood and roofing panels. Now it's a few shambly structures set back fifty metres from Playa Matina, a jungle-lined beach of black sand that stretches for miles. Walls are green, decorated with paintings of sea turtles. Showers are cold, the bogs fronted by curtains rather than doors. Two hours a day of electricity. Sea turtles? None. They stop turtles being poached and guard their eggs until they hatch, but have no turtles on site.

A schedule is written on a whiteboard:

Breakfast: 8am

Work: 9am - 11am

Lunch: 1pm

Work: 3pm - 5pm

Dinner: 7pm

Patrolling: From 8pm (4 Hour Shifts)

The first job is to move the "hatchery". It sounds as though it's a scientific building; theirs is a metre-high mound of sand the size of a badminton court. Eggs plucked from the beach are placed in the hatchery for safety for the time it takes them to hatch — about sixty days. If left on the beach, poachers steal the eggs and sell them. Sea turtles are an endangered species — even to touch one is illegal — but some restaurants offer them on the sly. People still eat the eggs and meat despite knowing they're endangered. Because people are idiots. Even Johnny — now a baseball-capped crusader against poaching — ate them as a child. "Kids here don't say 'cute' if you show them a photo of a sea turtle," says Barbara. "They say 'tasty'."

We're to shift the hatchery a metre and a half forward to freshen and loosen the sand used for last year. The Germans have been at it days, yet have done only 10% of the job. It's only sand, I think, I'll finish it by sunset. The Germans and I stand in a line, shovels flinging sand over our shoulders. I start off like I'm the Markimum Extreme Sand Shoveller v8. That lasts for a few minutes. I'm soon shagged. The sun burns my back and the shovel blisters my palms. I'd rather shift the sand with my bare hands, but don't want to look catlike, as if I'm covering an al fresco shite. To finish this today, I concede, is unrealistic — especially as I've never grafted a day in my life. My grandfather was a miner; my dad is an engineer; me, I'm lazy. I can't take a third toilet break, so slowly I slog on, daydreaming of a drawer of cocaine — powered by that, I'd have it done in an hour — and thinking that fifty hours of shovelling should be the sentence for theft or littering. Nothing would be stolen; the streets would be spotless. After an hour Barbara comes to see how we're doing. I ask, "Have you got any spreadsheets you need updating?" She hasn't. Isn't it odd, I think, as I toil on, that turtles take to land to lay eggs, then leave their babies forever. What if the first thing the babies see after they hatch is a dog? Wouldn't they think they too were dogs? If the first thing I saw was a turtle, I'd have spent my life living as a turtle. It may have been for the best.

After rice and beans, another session of shovelling, and more rice and beans, it's time for the night patrol. To avoid the heat and predators, sea turtles come ashore only during darkness. Our range is the four kilometres south of the refuge to the mouth of the Rio Matina, beyond which is Puerto Limon. Torches scare the turtles, so aren't allowed. And to merge with the scenery — again for the sake of the turtles — we're clad in black. Under the light of a half-moon, down the beach we march in a line, scanning the shoreline of the inky sea. As we go, tripping over a forest of driftwood — fallen trees bare of bark, washed down the river and out to sea, then back to shore. This debris — also rocks and trash — rules out flip-flops. I refused a pair of Crocs they offered, said I'll look like a div. And the wellies they had didn't fit me. So I wore Chelsea boots. When Johnny saw what I'm wearing, he laughed and started to salsa.

I see something in the distance, a black shape on the shore. I ask, "Is that one?"

Barbara says no.

Five minutes later: "There?" I say, pointing.

"No."

"That is, for sure," I say a minute later.

She says it isn't.

"It is," I insist.

"You can check if you want," she says.

I check; it's not.

"When you see one, you'll know," she says. "Their shells shine in the moonlight."

After fifteen minutes I ask, "What about that?"

"No."

I don't really know what I'm looking for: Is a sea turtle basically a tortoise that can swim? No, says Barbara. Sea turtles have flippers instead of feet, and they're a lot larger: Leatherbacks — one of the three types we hope to find, along with greens and hawksbills — measure up to two metres and can weigh as much as 500 kg.

No turtles so far, but we're not alone out here: Wraithlike faceless figures traipse to and fro. When we see one coming, we crouch in silence to avoid being spotted by the spectres. "Better to avoid confrontation," says Barbara. I agree, but have anyway armed myself with a club-shaped piece of wood to even the game: they have machetes. It's a public beach, unprotected, so poachers have as much right to be here as us. They can only be arrested if they're caught red-handed with a turtle or eggs, and there's a lot of beach and not a lot of police — we've seen none. Barbara says she and Johnny have an unwritten agreement with the poachers that equates to finders keepers.

"So if you see them pulling eggs from a nest," I say, "you just let them do it?"

"Yes."

It's not that they hate turtles; they're poaching to make meagre ends meet. Banana plantations are the primary employers in the region; for a 5am to 5pm shift, workers are paid a pittance: £2 an hour — and Costa Rica's the most expensive country in Central America. A week of poaching pays more than a month in the plantations, and the hours are shorter, the work less strenuous. So they must be peeved at the likes of the Krauts and me being here, pinching their egg-shaped salaries. They must think, *Haven't you got anything better to do than fanny about on this beach, stopping me earning for my family, just so you can tell your friends you're 'saving the planet'?*

Unfortunately for you, mate, no.

For three hours we walk and wait and walk and wait,

plod back and forth through the charcoal landscape. No nests. No turtles. No nothing. It's the arse end of saving the earth. For every photo of Greenpeace harpooning Japanese fishermen, there are a million tiresome moments of yawning tedium. On one of the waits, Maximo and I — who have split from the others to cover more ground — sit on a log and drink from coconuts, and stare into the starry sky, spotting constellations. I see a shooting star, the first I've ever seen. I wish to see a turtle, then curse the choice. If I'd wished for a million pounds I could've bought a turtle: kept it in the bath at home, looked at it whenever I wanted. Soon after, the walkie-talkie relays a message. "*Vamos,*" says Maximo, springing to his feet and breaking into a jog. "*Tortuga.*"

We run down the beach to meet Barbara and the Germans. "Where is it?" I pant to Barbara, out of breath.

"Shh." She points. I see it, a metre away. "It's a green turtle," she whispers. "A big one. If poachers found this, they would take the turtle as well as the eggs."

Using its flippers, it inches itself forward, scouting for a spot to drop its load. I will her on as she tries to lift herself up a sandy ledge. *Come on, love, heave. Three, two, one, heave.* She can't get up; it's too steep. She moves along the beach searching for a better place but has the same problem. After twenty minutes she tires and turns back to the sea. "She'll be back," says Barbara. "Tonight, or tomorrow, or later in the week." No eggs, but the sight of the turtle lights a fire within. I barely cared about turtles before; now I'm their saviour. Next town I'm at, on my back I'll get a full-size tattoo of a turtle shell.

It's not past midnight when the Germans say they're

tired and want to sleep. I'm keen to stay out, but even
Barbara isn't cheerleading for an all-nighter. "*Manana*," she
says. She's the boss; tomorrow then it is.

I've staged a strike. A lie-in, to be exact: I'm not getting out of
bed to work until the night patrols restart. The five days I've
been here, we're yet to clock an all-night patrol. The longest
patrol was four hours. The last two nights, we did none.
Since I came we've got one nest; poachers have claimed thirteen — we know the nests were there because each morning
Maximo walks the length of the beach to check. Most nests
were two to four kilometres down the beach. We've rarely
patrolled beyond a kilometre. Patrolling a quarter of the
range for less than half the time, it's no wonder we're being
trounced. Johnny and Barbara have gone AWOL, leaving us
short. I said I'd do it solo, stay up until 4am, but volunteers
aren't allowed to patrol without a worker. The final straw
was being told to rake leaves from a path no one uses and do
it while nests from last night remained unchecked — and
may still have eggs in them if poachers missed them. I
thought I'd be parading up and down the beach in a super-
hero costume, punching poachers. Here I am, though, doing
the work of a leaf-blower. Other tasks have also been of the
wax on, wax off variety: picking up trash, dehusking
coconuts, and, of course, shovelling a shitload of sand. It's
felt like a gulag. One I've paid to be at: £170 for a week. For
an endangered species, I expected urgency. I thought
through-the-night patrols would be sacrosanct. But at night
we're in bed — and no one ever found a turtle in their

bed. Fuck the leaves, I thought, and forget the hatchery. Feet on the beach should be the priority. So that's why I'm on strike.

And it works: The Germans too down tools, and hearing of the mutiny Johnny and Barbara return.

We set out to check a couple of nests I found this morning before I went on strike — Maximo had by then stopped his morning beach walks, so the score is likely worse than 13-1. A nest is a lumpy circle, a circumference of several metres; leading to it from the sea, a track resembling that of a tractor tyre. Easy to see, but the eggs are deep down, and could be anywhere within the circle. Johnny stands with hand to chin, then pokes a metre-long stick into the sand. It's a miss. He tries again. A miss. And again. Miss. At first the pokes appear reasoned, but by the tenth time it's random. At last a smile follows the strike. He draws the stick from the sand; from the end of it drips a yolky yellow. Barbara lays face down and scoops sand from the spot. A metre below the surface is a cavern. She pulls on a white latex glove and pulls out the eggs, delicately placing them in a sack: "Two . . . twelve . . . twenty . . ." I peer into the nest; there are loads left. ". . . sixty-two . . . seventy-four . . . eighty-eight, and one more makes eighty-nine." A lot from one animal in one go, I think, but, says Barbara, "This is average."

I ask, "What's the price for an egg?"

"A dollar," she says. "Two for a big one."

That's more than I thought. I might swap sides.

Johnny ties a knot in the top of the sack, then tries to hand it to me. Worried I'll drop the sack, I say no. He insists, though, saying it's "my nest". It's heavy, with not just the eggs in the sack but sand too. I carry it back to the refuge, stopping for regular breaks. If I had to carry this bag for nine months, I'd be down the clinic at sunrise.

The hatchery is a decade from being finished, so we'll bury the eggs in the sand in front. Barbara uses her arm like a flipper to make a nest the depth and dimensions of the original. "Mark, it's your nest," she says, rising, "you can put in the eggs." It's tough being a parent, non-stop. I lay down by the hole and dip my hand into the sack. I pull out two eggs, the size and weight of a chicken's, soft-shelled and circular. Under the red glow of Barbara's headlamp, I softly place them into the hole, naming them as I go: *Michelangelo and Donatello, Raphael and Leonardo, Bowser and Kermit* — he's a frog, but they're both green, and I need a lot of names. "Now fill it with sand," says Barbara. "Make it compact, to keep out the rain." Nothing but work, these bastards. But I love 'em, every last one.

Job done, I stand and reflect that I've just added eighty-nine endangered animals into the world. If half of those are female and each of those has eighty-nine eggs, and half of those are female and each of those has eighty-nine eggs, twenty years from now I can claim credit for an extra hundred thousand turtles in the sea. That, though, is overly optimistic. The likelihood is that none of these eggs will grow into adults. Only 60% hatch. Of those, one in a thousand survives the ten years it takes to reach adulthood. The rest are eaten by predators while they're small or die from fishing or pollution. So more likely than an extra hundred thousand turtles is a 10% chance that one extra adult turtle will be alive. Not as impressive sounding, so at dinner parties I'll use the larger but less accurate number.

With the two nests checked — the other had been raided by a poacher — we start to patrol. Conditions hinder us: clouds cover the moon; rain falls and the wind howls. Visibility is almost zilch. Where was Puerto Limon is now nothing. When I fall a few metres behind Gerardo, he too disappears. But on we go, up and down the black beach. Twelve kilometres we walk for no returns, spirits breaking like the unruly waves. At 2am I'm sat on a trunk with Gerardo beneath a wringing blanket of blackness, clothes as drenched as if I'd worn them in the shower. My already sodden boots were soaked further by an inrush of the wild sea. I take one off and turn it upside down; water pours from it like a tap. No one said this would be glamorous, I think, head in my hands, but no one said it would be so grim. It's insane, crazy, mad; like looking for needles in a haystack — blindfolded. Easier, surely, to pay poachers for the eggs they find: For the £700 the Germans and I paid for this week, Barbara could have bought ten nests — eight more than we've got. As well as insane, practically pointless. Last year the refuge released six thousand babies into the sea. Six of those will survive long-term. Scant reward for the time and effort and expense. And while they're endangered, there are still hundreds of thousands of sea turtles — whereas there are only a couple of thousand pandas. And if they go extinct, so what? Boohoo. We lost the dodo, the dinosaurs, Princess Diana too, and still the earth spins.

PUERTO VIEJO

"Ow yuh doing?" says a fella with short dreads and an oversized crochet beanie, as I go to sit on a bench beside a palmy beach.

"Good," I say. "Just here to sit and eat these peanuts." I hold up the bag to show him.

"Let's eat, mon. Mi name Ralcetin." He holds out his fist for me to bump.

We sit. I tip some peanuts into his hand.

"Weh yuh fram?" he says. "England, rite?"

"Yeah. Birmingham."

"Suh yuh know UB40?"

I nod.

"Mi use to play wid Ali Campbell an dem boys in Birmingham an Brixton, an wen dey cum Jamaica." He talks about this for a couple of minutes, then says, "Now, yuh looking fah ah likle someting fah put up yuh nose?"

I tell him I'm not.

"Yuh du nah like to sniff? Dis stuff just cum fram Colombia." He taps his watch. "Tree forty-five dis mawnin de boat cum in, just here." He points at the sea in front.

I raise an eyebrow.

"Ah true, mon. Fresh stuff dis."

I say, "It's Wednesday, nothing's happening, so it's pointless buying some."

"Does nah matta wat day tis. Everi day ah gud day fah ah bit of blo."

"How much is it?"

"Sixty dolla."

"That's the same as it costs in Birmingham."

"Ah nah de siem ah dat shit inna England, dat dey cut wid everyting. Dis 95% pure, mon. Yuh affi push real hawd to crush dis." He makes a grinding gesture with his thumb.

I tell him I'll think about it.

He says, "Ow bout ah donation? Mi saving fah ah jerk chicken pan."

"A what?"

"Ah jerk chicken pan. Yuh know, ah pan fah cooking jerk chicken. Mi guh na put it rite dere, yuh know, an cook jerk chicken." He thumbs over his shoulder towards the road. "Mi had one before but de sea cum up an tek it."

A guy comes, tokes a pretend spliff. I tell him no thanks. "Gi mi mon here som peanuts," says Ralcetin, nodding at the skunk seller. I tip some in his hand. He walks away.

"Bout dis donation," says Ralcetin, "ten dolla, twenty dolla, whateva yuh can giv."

"I'm not giving ten dollars to someone I don't know."

"Five dolla, it ok. Depend pon yuh budget. Yuh gi mi five dolla, tomorrow mi buy de wheel fah mi pan. Mi bredren mek it now, but him had to stop cah de money run out, yuh know."

"Can't you use the money from selling coke to pay for the pan?"

"Yuh see, mi ave two pots," — he makes a circle with his hand to the left, then a second to the right — "an de money fram sell de stuff mi put inna dis pot," — he points to the left — "an mi use dat fah me food an dat. An de money fram donations me put inna dis pot," — he points to the right — "an me use dat fah fi mi pan."

"That's a great plan," I tell him, "but, really, I don't give money to people I don't know."

"Mi nah ah nobody. Mi just said dat mi know dem boys fram UB40, didn't mi? An yuh be fram Birmingham."

"If you're friends with Ali Campbell, why not ask him to pay for your jerk chicken pan?"

"But dem boys ova deh, nah here. Ow mi guh na ask him? Me ave nah gat iz numba nuh mo."

"I'm sure UB40 have a Facebook page. You could message Ali Campbell about your pan."

We talk a minute more, and then I use the empty bag of peanuts as my excuse to leave.

He fits the scene of rough-edged Puerto Viejo, a lazy town with scruffy charm on Costa Rica's Caribbean coastline — in the south-east of the country, 40 km from Panama. Rasta red, green, and yellow are rife, as are braids, dreads, tattoos. Butch blokes shoot hoops and lean on lampposts catching tourist eyes with split-second-too-long glances: "Yuh want som smoke?" Kids flip tricks at a skate-ramp tacked onto a church, and cacao and mangoes and banana bread sold on the beach beside upturned beaten boats.

Some camp on the sand, cooking on coals next to their tent or van. Others booze in bars: expats escaping winters, student loans, unwanted children.

Twelve kilometres of jungle-backed, golden-bronze beaches stretch south from Puerto Viejo; palm-fringed paradises, the sandy-coved, clear-watered Caribbean of high-street brochures. No resorts, no condos; for long stretches, not even people. Playa Cocles attracts the largest crowd: bodies and weed burn, wild waves are surfed: I want to try, and speak to a guy sat by a shack beside a rack of boards. He asks if I've surfed before.

I say I haven't.

"Have a lesson," he says. "Only £40."

"How much to just hire a board?"

"£3 an hour."

If it takes me ten hours to teach myself, I'll save £10; so I tell him, "I'll teach myself. It can't be that hard."

"You'll have to stay near the shore, like that guy." He points at a bloke flapping around in water that's knee-deep, a few metres from the shore.

I don't want to be *that* guy. And as I walk away, and see one of the many bikini-clad cyclists that ply the road to and from Puerto Viejo, I'm reminded that I should get my priorities straight: bicycle before surfboard. I never learnt to ride one when I was four or five, even nine or ten, and then I was at an age where I was too self-conscious. But I wish I'd bit the bullet back then. At twelve it's not cool, at thirty-five it's comical — someone will video me, and I'll go viral. I'll wait until I've had a stroke; then I can claim I could before but am having to relearn.

Near Playa Cocles, ringed by pristine rainforest, is the

Jaguar Rescue Center. It's named in honour of the original animal brought to the centre. Now they rescue all kinds of wildlife but have no jaguars. It's a drop-in visit for me — no more volunteering. I've done my bit for the earth: one hundred thousand sea turtles. Plus I turn off lights when I leave a room and I rarely piss in the sea: isn't that enough? Animals are in pens or behind screens or bars, but it's not like a zoo. They're in their natural habitat and show no signs of stress. Some even roam free, like a deer, a pelican, a peccary. A chance to see animals close up without contributing to their exploitation. Visitors actually contribute to their rehabilitation: The entry fee — £15 per person — is reinvested in the centre and helps it achieve a fifty-plus percent release rate for the 600-or-so injured or orphaned animals that come to it per year. "We love these animals," says Dan, one of the red-shirted, jolly-faced volunteers giving the tours, "but if we think they can survive in the wild, we let them go."

"Animals end up here for four reasons," says Dan, as he walks us along one of the leafy paths that criss-cross the centre, dividing the enclosures. "People, people, people, and people. Firstly, people get dogs but then don't take care of them; they're let loose, live wild. The mouth of a dog in Costa Rica is disgusting; it's basically venomous. If they attack an animal, we need to receive it within a few hours; if not, we have to put down the animal; already the infection has spread too far. Reason number two, the insulation on power lines wears off after four years, and people are too poor or too lazy to fix it. Animals that touch the lines die 99% of the time; we get the babies — baby sloths, baby monkeys — that were holding onto mom when she grabbed the cable. Third reason, some see a wild animal and think they can make a lot of money from it, selling it abroad; those saved from the black market are given to us. Fourth, the trash people dump by the side of the road attracts insects, which attract rats, mice, lizards, small birds, and they attract snakes, wild cats, birds of prey; and when they come onto the road, they get hit by cars."

Dan shows us a margay named Little Devil, a type of wild cat that's twice the size of a house cat. He says, "Twice we've tried and failed to release Little Devil. First time he came back with a face full of porcupine spikes; he tried to kill the wrong animal. Second time he came back at night and decided it's not a rescue centre but a restaurant. One owl, one anteater, and the ear of a monkey." That's not how he got his name, though: "A friend of the owner came from Barcelona Zoo. He said, 'I work with big cats — lions, tigers, jaguars, leopards — I can go inside with a small cat.' It took three men with sticks to get Little Devil off his face."

As we pass the birds of prey, several of which are owls, Dan says, "People think owls are smart; those big, wise eyes that peer into your soul. Those eyes, though, take up two-thirds of an owl's skull. There's not much room left for brain. To assess the intelligence of birds, there's a test: show food to one, then put a cup over the food. Ravens and crows, highly intelligent, knock over the cup. Hawks and eagles use blunt force to break the cup. Owls don't do anything. The second you put a cup over the food, they think, *Oh, the food has gone.*"

Next Dan shows us Coco the one-eyed crocodile — a man beat it with a metal pipe, hoping to take its tail to use as an aphrodisiac — and a family of sloths huddled upside down on a tree, and a large wicker basket of baby sloths, and dozens of snakes. He tells us there are 145 snake species in Costa Rica, and that 24 of those are venomous. Depending on the snake, the venom will attack your central nervous system or clot your blood. He points at one of the snakes: "Here's a baby, baby, baby boa constrictor. Emphasis on *baby* because adult ones can grow to be five metres. They wrap tightly around their prey, squeeze the life out of it. As an adult you're too large for it to attack — but don't let your child near one."

The centre has lots of monkeys: spider monkeys, howler monkeys, capuchin monkeys. Dan says, "We had one capuchin monkey that wanted to dig for insects. It tried to use a big stick, but the stick was too heavy for it to use. It dragged the stick to me and placed it in my hands, then made back and forth movements with its hands while looking at me, to show me what to do. If an animal can use a tool, it's a sign of intelligence; if it can teach another species how to use a tool, that's amazing. I had goosebumps, and tears in my eyes, as I stood digging a hole for a monkey."

I'm staying at Playa 506, a hostel on Playa Cocles: beach-front with deckchairs, craft beers and a chill crowd. Guests and staff and a bunch of friends of the barman gather on the beach for a bonfire and *rondon* (a spicy stew). Busy hands chop and slice and grind, then fire-lit faces are at it like witches, adding veggies and heads of fish and hearts of chil-dren to a cauldron-like charred vessel fuelled by driftwood, stirring, stirring, stirring the bubbling, frothing broth, then leaving it to simmer, a rubbery fishy eye staring from within. It's spooned into large bowls, and around the bonfire we sit like hobos, scoffing, swigging, smoking.

One of the guests is Mike: fortyish with a ponytail and baseball cap backwards; friendly, polite, but with an if-you-mess-with-me-I-will-fuck-you-up edge. When I ask how long he's been travelling, he says he's not. "I can't go back to the States. Shit went down a couple of years ago. Better I don't talk about it."

A few beers later he tells more: "They got me on the Patriot Act."

I say, "Isn't that for terrorists?"

"Supposed to be."

"So how have they got you on that?"

"Fucking dirty cops in Texas. Corrupt they are, caught up in all sorts. They killed a couple of my buddies. Can't let shit like that go. So I started making bombs, was gonna blow up some shit."

"But you didn't?"

"Nah, I didn't; they were on to me. It would be at least twenty years in jail, so I got out over the border to Mexico."

"And just kept going?"

"Nothing else to do but that."

"You've had no problems crossing borders?"

"Ain't crossed none of them officially."

I hang out by the fire until midnight, then my dormmate John and I return to our room. He's bearded and tattooed, an Irish-blooded American, an Alaskan fisherman by trade; a bottle-of-liquor-a-day, seven-phones-a-year kind of guy who carries around a book called *101 Places To Get Fucked Up Before You Die* like he's a priest and it's his bible. At the room, which only he and I are sharing, he pulls out a bag of coke and racks rails on his iPad. He says, "I bought it for fifteen bucks from one of those guys in town." He sniffs a line, then holds out the iPad. "Have a bump."

I know I shouldn't — drugs are bad, and all that — but I've been ill in bed the last few days, and am celebrating being alive. By the third day I was sure I had malaria. I searched "Costa Rica malaria" and learnt there was an outbreak at the end of last year. Three places were hit, one of which was Matina de Limon. Then I was sure it was malaria. But I ate some French fries and felt better, so either I didn't have malaria or the cure for malaria is French fries.

I take the iPad, take the note. *Snniiiffff.* An orgasm on Christmas morning: that feeling distilled, pumped into my head like petrol and set ablaze. Sprawled on our beds, shirt-less and sweating and pop-eyed, our sweetly-numbed tongues compress a month's worth of conversation into a few hours. We sniff and talk, talk and drink, talk of life and loss, of broken hearts and bucket-lists, of the rights and wrongs of the world. In sync and on song — until 3am, when the coke has gone.

"That's that then," I say. "Time to sleep."

"Yep," he says. "Sleep."

Of that, though, there's no chance. I'll have completed Netflix before I'll be able to sleep. I know he feels the same. I also know he has the same idea as me — anyone coked with their stash run dry has this idea. We're both waiting for the other one to say it.

At last I say, "Do you reckon—"

"Reckon," he says, "we should get some more blow?"

"Yeah."

"Do you think there will still be someone selling?"

"Probably not. It's 3am."

"I don't think so either. But . . ."

"Want to go check?"

"Yeah."

"Let's go."

High as we are, we both know it's a bad idea. I even say it — "This is a bad idea." — on the twenty-minute troop into town. "Yeah, it is," he says. "Bad." But we walk on, slaves to our noses.

Everywhere in Puerto Viejo is closed. All lights are out. Only a few are about, dodgy or drunk or both. "I'll speak to this guy," says John; he crosses the street to speak to a loiterer with cornrows and a holey t-shirt — a sketchy-looking scoundrel best swerved under any circumstance but this. They chat for a minute then start to walk off. John gives me a signal to follow. When I catch up he tells me, "He hasn't got any, but he knows a man who has."

We walk to the end of the street. "Bak inna five," says Cornrows, then he walks down a side street.

John and I sit on the kerb. He's edgy, and he's not a man easily unnerved. "I've got bad vibes about this," he says. "We should leave."

I'm also not keen on the vibe, but I want that coke. I say, "Let's give it a minute."

We sit a few minutes longer, then start down the street back to where we came from. Half a minute later there's a shout from behind: Cornrows; he jogs our way. John and I walk back to him. As we meet, a truck roars up from behind and screeches to a stop. Four cops leap out, yelling Spanish and flashing lights in our faces. We put our hands in the air. They take each of us to a corner of the truck to be searched. I'm too wired to be stressed, though I recognise the seriousness. The cop on me rifles roughly through my pockets and inspects my wallet, tears apart a pack of gum I have. He pats along my arms and legs, runs his thumb around the waistline of my boxers, jiggles my crotch through my jeans. I've had sex that was less intimate. Then he spends a minute scanning the ground for anything I might have discarded. Finding nothing, he motions me to go. John is still being searched; I wait for him to be given the clear, then we walk away. Cornrows is still at the truck; his stuff spread in the back of it. The wrap of coke is open.

A lucky escape. Seconds later and that coke would have been in our hands not his, and we would have been screwed. Fucking stupid to come out at this time to score coke. Lesson learned — for all of three minutes: "See that bloke there," I say, still craving, "let's ask him."

PANAMA CITY

Skyscrapers soaring across the skyline, a slew of malls and casinos, a Hard Rock Hotel, a Hooters. Cinta Costera, a palm-lined promenade, connects the gleaming present to the past: Casco Viejo, a pastel-hued Spanish-influenced neighbourhood on a peninsula jutting into the Pacific. Few above three storeys compared to few below thirty across the bay. Casco Viejo was the city, then came the cash and it was left to rot: graffiti covered the walls, gangs colonised the buildings. The ghetto was recently gentrified — out with the gangs, in with gelato — and now Casco Viejo is tailor-made for Instagram: renovated churches, age-old ramparts, prissy facades, shady plazas. A shareable snapshot. But the story is a site with no soul. Overrun with sweaty, slurping cruise-shippers on day-release from their cocoons of gluttony. Herded like kids on a field trip, these infantilised fatheads — sandals with socks, wide brim sun hats; slung about their necks, cameras bigger than their brains — shuffle around the bubble-wrapped experience swigging cans of Coke and

swiping credit cards at stores stocked with Panama hats —
which in Panama, I suppose, are simply called hats.

Nice, yes; but fake, a sham. Real is the larger abutting
neighbourhoods of El Chorrillo and Santa Ana. A couple of
blocks of transition, where the underclass and the bourgeois
live side by side or face off over the road — and is a sign
painted on a bed-sheet: "Stop the gentrification"; and bill-
boards declaring development is on the way, showing
pictures of how it will look, so different to the now to be
reinvention not renovation — then it's like day to night.
Tumbledown tenements mingled with crumbling colonial-
ism, frayed antiques constructed exquisitely — arched
windows, ornate balconies, touches of stucco — before
being left to slide. Lines aslant and angles askew; paint
peeled and smudged with mould. Facades that are just that
and no more. Through gaping holes where should be doors
and windows: nothing; no floors, no stairs, no walls. To call
them a house is like calling a pair of socks an outfit. But here
life is seen; unlike Casco Viejo, where are only hints at lives
being lived, where in windows nothing moves. Here life is
laid bare, is a sense of community. Doors open, dwellers
lazing within, gossiping in shadowy interiors. Washing on
balconies, women with hair in rollers nattering between
upstairs windows. Checkers played with bottle tops, ping-
pong on a table made from crates — the net a plank of
wood. A washing machine roadside for sale (£12); atop it a
toilet brush in holder (no price stated). "*Cristo Vive*" sprayed
in red on a wall — "Christ Lives". Character that's lost when
buildings are made-over, residents transplanted. Because
places don't have character; people do. Take the people from
a place, and it loses its character. Casco Viejo has lost its.

But with real comes risk, comes riffraff and ruffians loitering in the street, draped on discarded furniture. A scowling cluster shoot me a sharp stare. I hesitate but continue. Until a block on when I'm warned not to go further. "It's not safe," a man tells me. "The police, even they don't come here."

From Santa Ana I walk to Caledonia, several kilometres along Avenida Central, a hodgepodge high street of over-flowing rubbish bins, of stores selling phone covers, of pouty-mouthed, trashy-clothed mannequins. Watermelons and tomatoes sold from crates; beside tables of bruised bananas, women selling lottery tickets from briefcases. Stools along counter windows at hole-in-the-wall eateries; diners tucking into fried-up, dried-up dishes. Metal doors and blacked-out windows, grotty hotels that rent rooms for an hour. Reggaeton pounds, neon lights flash. Every fifth store is a "Mini Super": sadly-lit with tired fans and half-empty shelves of knock-off brands. All of them run by Chinese; many of the cafes as well, serving fried rice and chow mein. They're everywhere, the Chinese. There's talk of starting a colony on Mars; we'll get there and find there's already a Chinatown.

Every city is nuanced, but nuance takes time, and labels don't. So we stick labels on places. Panama City: skyscrapers, wealthy, canal. That veneer covers the coastline; that's what you see in the tourist board photos. But as a person isn't their profile photo, a destination isn't its brochure. As for guidebooks, they're the résumé of a place. And you should never believe a résumé. A résumé doesn't mention a person's divorce, alcoholism, schizophrenia — if it does it's the résumé of someone unemployed. The truth of a place is its parts not advertised nor photographed. Santa Ana, Caledonia, El Chorrillo: this is the majority and thus the truth. But they're unseen by those who visit this city. Visitors — to here, to anywhere — want the idea of a place, turn a blind eye to all else. They prefer prettified and polished: the old town, the historic quarter, confection like Casco Viejo; and the shiny and familiar, Starbucks and Hilton. They don't want real, don't want truth. They want simply to say that they've been — and have selfies to show for it. Because where they've visited says as much about them as the brands they wear, the postcode they live in.

Whatever Panama City is, it's more prosperous than its Central American brothers. It has its canal to thank. I visit the locks at Miraflores: the Pacific entrance and exit to the canal that bisects Panama at its narrowest point — the narrowest point of the continent — to unite the Pacific and the Atlantic. An engineering marvel to match the pyramids, so they say. But here at Miraflores it's not much to look at: a few locks, a couple of channels of green water. A few men in hard hats walk about; none rush nor shout. To the right, in a small lake, cruise liners and cargo ships and tankers waiting their turn, some of the forty a day that transit the canal — from the Pacific toward the Atlantic in the morning, the reverse in the afternoon.

From here to the Atlantic it's eighty kilometres through what was once solid earth. The French first had a go at carving a waterway through the country; they wrote it off after twenty years, defeated by finances and disease. 20,000 workers killed, mainly from malaria and yellow fever. A further 6,000 died during the successful endeavour by the US from 1904 to 1914. Having built it, the

Americans had the rights to it. The Canal Zone was closed to Panamanians, was in all but name a colony: militarised, Stars and Stripes flying; US-run schools, churches, golf clubs. In 1977 the US agreed to hand over the canal — twenty-two years later. The effort and expense to construct the canal are why it costs so much to use it: as much as £200,000. The alternative is a 15,000-kilometre two-week detour around Cape Horn, the southern extreme of the continent.

Locks are needed because of mountains in the middle of the country; on entry to the canal they raise ships to the level of dam-created Lake Gatun — 26 metres above sea level and the longest section of the canal — then on exit lower them back to sea level. At Miraflores — one of three sets of locks in the canal — ships are lifted or lowered 16.5 metres in two stages. The additional 9.5 metres is done at other locks, 4 km from here. First to the locks is a cargo ship: the Cristina Star. 243.1 metres long, 32.2 metres wide, says an announcer in the viewing gallery I watch from. On each side of the locks on rails are small locomotives, connected by chains to the ship — their purpose to tow the freighter through the locks, keeping it correctly aligned. The locks are 33.5 metres wide — half a metre to spare on each side. The ship enters the locks; the gate at the rear of it closes. Ahead of it a drop at least two storeys. Water drains from the first chamber into the second. The ship sinks, slowly, so slowly, almost imperceptibly. When the water levels between its current chamber and the next are level, the gate in front opens; the ship eases into the next chamber; the gate behind closes. Water is again drained, and the freighter again falls. When it's level with the sea, the gate ahead opens and the ship floats into the Pacific, completing its ten-hour cruise across Panama.

In; out; next. Simple, so it seems. But make no mistake, it's a manmade miracle, this lifting and lowering of whopping vessels, this threading of behemoths through the eyes of needles, and manoeuvring them through mountains. And in the distance an even greater spectacle: the newly-opened extension to the canal, which handles ships three times the size of these. The Cristina Star is a tiddler to the one I see there, crawling through the countryside.

Next into the locks is a cruise liner: the Celebrity Infinity. They wave at us like they're royalty. These make-believe queens and kings are a captive market for a mooning. No one else is keen, though, except for one boy, and if it's just him and me with our ass out, well, it's weird. Those on the cruise are one and the same with the vacuous waddlers I saw at Casco Viejo. Here too they are, in the viewing gallery, burger-bloated bottoms on bleachers, guzzling Gatorade and gorging on Pringles. Selfie sticks in front of selfie sticks in front of selfie sticks, trying to fit in the huge ships as well as their fat heads.

One bloke, though, is atypical: Thor, in his sixties, sporting a ponytail beneath his balding bonce and red specs across his tight face. He looks frazzled, as if he's been electrocuted, and shakily clasps a ring binder of paperwork. He asks where I'm from. I tell him, then return the question.

"I'm not from anywhere," he says. "I'm a free citizen."

"But you're from somewhere."

"I've lived in Cuba for the last three years."

"But you're not Cuban, are you?"

"No."

"Where were you born?"

"Norway."

"So you're Norwegian?"

"I'm not, so say the Norwegian government. I'm called Thor, I speak Norwegian, but I'm not Norwegian? The stupid bastards."

He concedes that he's had Canadian citizenship for fourteen years. He married — then later divorced — a Canadian and lived there and got citizenship, but Norway doesn't allow you to be a citizen of another country unless you give up your Norwegian citizenship. He secretly held onto his, but the Norwegian authorities recently realised and revoked his passport. Now he's in the process of annulling his Canadian citizenship while reapplying to be Norwegian and trying to obtain a residence permit for Cuba.

He says, "I have to deal with three embassies. A mess it is, a joke. My ancestors were Vikings; do you think they asked to go places? Did they fuck. They just went."

I suggest that Canada is an alright country, that he could make do with that citizenship.

He's infuriated. "People think Canada is an oh-so-nice country, but it's not. It doesn't give any money to its citizens. Western political bastards. Fuckers, all of them. They're all corrupt." Then he dissolves into largely incoherent mutterings about conspiracies.

From what I gather, the reason he now wants to revert to being Norwegian is basically because of money: he's entitled to more as a Norwegian than as a Canadian.

He says he's just been to the Norwegian consulate. "They don't even speak fucking Norwegian. They said they can't help. They told me to go to fucking Colombia."

"So you'll go to Colombia?"

"I'm not going to fucking Colombia."

"What then?"

"I have a bit of marijuana; I'll smoke that and have a think about what to do."

He also tells me: "In Cuba I have a couple of girlfriends. One's twenty-two; the other's twenty-nine. Sisters. I live with their grandmother; she wants me to marry them. And I know this other woman in Ukraine; she said 'Thor, a man like you needs many wives.' She sent some sexy pics. I'll show you."

Abroad it's easier to get away with being a loon. Hundreds of thousands are at large overseas, incensed, jabbering. Typically divorced with children they don't see, and a penchant for cigarettes and alcohol and drugs, and a personal vendetta against seven billion people.

I need a ship for the next leg of the trip. From Prudhoe Bay in northern Alaska to Ushuaia at the foot of Argentina, the Pan-American Highway provides 30,000 kilometres unbroken transit through fourteen countries — except for a hundred kilometres between Panama and Colombia: the infamous Darien Gap. The jungly, swampy wilderness is one of the most gnarly and lawless regions on the planet, the domain of narcos and FARC guerrillas. I can't go through, so I'll go around.

I spoke to an agent who told me a few yachts were sailing to Colombia this week and recommended one called Victory. She said, "It won the Admiral's Cup."

Sounds decent, I thought. I'll take that.

"In 1981," she added.

Which is like saying you can sleep with the winner of

Miss World 1981. Great in 1981; not so great in 2018 when she's fifty-eight.

The agent gave the names of some other ships, which I researched. Reviews were mixed: there was talk of inept captains; captains abusive, insane, drunk, high. And talk of boats being past-their-best and overcrowded. I gambled on one called Big Fish II. At £400 it's pricier than flying, but flights are instantly forgettable, and five days on a yacht sailing from Panama to Colombia, with a stop-off at the San Blas Islands, will one way or another be unforgettable.

A couple of hours from Panama City is Puerto Lindo, a fishing village on the Caribbean coastline. There, as the sun sets, I board the Big Fish II: a white yacht five metres across, thirteen metres long. As compact as a caravan, to be shared for several days with several strangers: Sam and Sarah, a couple from Australia, twenty-six years old; Lilly, thirty-three, from Greece, and Lucie from Switzerland and Benny from Germany — both twenty, on a gap year. Jarri, the captain, and Luis, the first mate, are Colombian, in their mid-twenties. Francia is French and the cook, and the only English speaker of the three. She's an olive-skinned, curly-haired Parisian; about thirty but has the face of an impish child. She wears a skimpy bikini, has on her back a large tattoo of Ganesh. Her nails are red; orange beaded bracelets encircle her wrists. She smokes roll-ups and sucks lollipops. She calls people "Darling".

As Jarri and Luis push, spin, pull, tie — both their hands and feet at work — Francia shows us the boat. On the flat-top front, two sails large and triangular, and dozens of cables and ropes. The rear third is uncovered: two wheels for steering, nets of onions and oranges, a motor dinghy strung above an icebox. Padded vinyl seats and two thin tables stretch from the rear into the covered kitchen: a fridge and an oven, a sink and a spice rack, a retro laptop for navigation. Things fold up, others down or out; everything is locked in place. A few steps down from the kitchen are two toilets the size and style of those on planes, and four cabins little larger than an average ensuite. A "double bed" in each cabin, the size of an off-boat single; and in two of them a coffin-width "single" above the double — shelf-like.

I'll share a "triple cabin" with Benny. It's a squeeze for the two of us, never mind the three it's for. If it were a cell in a prison, it would breach human rights. I'd like the double bed, but don't accept when Benny offers to let me have it. He's offered because he thinks I'm old. To a twenty-year-old, I suppose I am. "We'll flip a coin," I say. I call heads. Twice I drop the coin, unbalanced by the swaying of the yacht. Third time it's tails. He again offers me the double. I tell him, "No, the coin has spoken." He won't have the double all to himself, though; he'll be sharing it with a surfboard. Sam — shoulder-length blonde hair, backwards baseball cap — brought it with him from Australia. He says, "Bit of an inconvenience, but better than using the crappy for-hire boards. I get some weird looks taking it on buses and showing up with it at places hundreds of miles from the sea. I see people thinking, *Why's that bloke brought a surfboard into the jungle?*"

After we've unpacked, Francia gathers us for a safety rundown, dos and don'ts mainly regarding switches and buttons. "This switch is for navigation. Never turn it off. Very important." And: "This here," — indicating an orange device, a Spot Gen3 — "is connected to the authorities. If you press this, boats and planes will come. The fine is $350,000. You press it, you pay." She says if we need fresh water — which is to be conserved — to press the red switch, and that the blue one is for sea water. She presses the blue one; a pump starts. "Don't leave it on," she says. "The boat will explode."

Later I'm laid in bed, nose an inch from the ceiling, sweating like a sow in a slaughterhouse. I'm on the verge of vomiting, nauseous from the constant rocking. I try to keep it down until I remember Francia's advice: "Better out than in." I stagger to spew HQ, off the back of the boat. I sit on the icebox, turn my head: *phurgh*. Jarri grins down at me from his stool at the wheel. No doubt thinks I'm a lightweight landlubber. No doubt he's right.

SAN BLAS ISLANDS

In bed, I turn my head, peer out the porthole: paradise. An idyllic island ringed by coral reef and hues of blues and greens. Silvery shoals of several hundred, a shipwreck in the shallows. I take to the deck to see a palm-speckled constellation of heavenly islands, on them nowt but a hut or two, roofed with feathery fronds. That one has only a hammock strung between its palms; that one not even a hammock. We anchor near one called Chichime. Francia says we can swim ashore — and reminds us not to flush the toilet if anyone is near the boat: "What you flush goes into the sea; no one snorkelling wants to see that." I pull on some shorts — well-worn Nikes from a Panama City thrift store — and swim to the island through water that's warm as a bath, as clear as gin, to sand so fine, so white, sugar-like.

Set back from the shore is a cluster of rudimentary thatch-roof shacks with skew-whiff bamboo walls slit like combs. In front are midget women that are part gypsy, part Oompa Loompa: crop-haired and wearing headscarves, loops of gold in their ears and septum, psychedelic patterns woven into their blouses, calves and forearms bound in bright bands of glass beads. Beside them some men; they wear jeans or shorts, vests or t-shirts — one only pants. The men are just as short, and short means very short: the Gunas, the indigenous inhabitants of this 370-island archipelago off Panama's Caribbean coast, are the second-shortest people in the world after the Pygmies of Africa. They have near-complete autonomy over their territory — which they call Guna Yala not San Blas. Part of Panama, but with their own flag, language, constitution. Outsiders — which includes Panamanians — can't buy land or invest in Guna Yala, or even settle long-term on the islands. And so insular are they, that if a Guna marries a non-Guna, the Guna is expelled from Guna Yala. All this with sound reason: it was foreigners who massacred them in the 16th century, foreigners who forced them to abandon the main-land. Once bitten, . . .

I laze first, roast beneath blueness whisked with white; then I wander, skirting the shoreline. A sandy footpath, a few more shacks: that's all that's here. Little Corn is a metropolis in comparison, its shops and school and side-walk and electricity. A few other boats are offshore; like ours, they're small sailboats. Cruise liners don't come to San Blas, kept away by the water being too shallow. Also no jet skis, parasails, scuba divers. I see guys harvesting coconuts from swaying palms, piling them in mounds; they sell them to tourists for a dollar. Francia told us not to take any stray ones we find, said that every coconut belongs to someone, even those on vacant islands. She said until the late 1990s coconuts were their principal currency. Gunas also earn from charging sailboats a couple of dollars per person to anchor at an island, and from photos — a dollar if you want a snap of them — and from fish and beer and *molas* (place-mat-sized hand-stitched patterns, the same as those on the women's blouses). A dollar here, two dollars there, twenty for a mola or a fish, is enough to survive, to support their peasant lifestyle.

Happy, so they seem, lazing in hammocks, admiring the luscious scenery — happier than the average woman on the Tube, fella in an office. It's good that they like it: to leave the region requires permission from a committee and it's rarely granted, says Francia when we're back on the boat, sailing to another island. She's dancing to the sounds of samba and salsa, sipping passion fruit and rum from a carved-out lemon. "One time we took one of the Gunas with us to Carta-gena — the city in Colombia where we dock. He kept saying he wanted to come, so one day we said, ok, come, thinking he would back out, but he didn't. Because he had no passport, we smuggled him into Colombia." She stubs her fag out in one of the beer cans taped around the boat to use as ashtrays. "We lent him shoes and clothes and took him to get a trendy haircut. Then we hired a taxi to show him the city, but it being his first time in a car, it made him feel sick. So we walked instead. His eyes popped with excitement. He couldn't believe such a place existed. In restaurants he ate with his hands; at bars he was so randy, seeing women dressed so sexily. He didn't want to leave, but he had to: his family, his house, his life is on the islands. The committee somehow learned about the trip and fined him £40. He didn't care: with the stories he had to tell, he was a superstar."

We anchor off Akuadargana: 200 metres long, 25 metres across; sand and palms and a couple of shacks, home to a handful of people — caretakers not owners, explains Francia. All the islands belong to the community; a family stays on one for six months then moves back to a village island and is replaced by another family.

"These village islands, where are they?" I ask.

Clustered closer to the mangrove-lined mountainous mainland, she tells me. That's where most of the 30,000 Gunas live. Life there isn't so idyllic: 1,000-plus people tightly packed; trash and rules and jobs.

I ask about the kids on this island, one of whom is playing keepy-uppy: "Do they go to school? What about children on other far-off islands?"

"Yes," says Francia, "they go to school on the village islands."

"Someone takes them there? Every day?"

"If they have family there they can live with, they stay for a week or two at a time."

"And if they have no family there?"

"They skip school for six months."

Doesn't matter really: a BSc (Hons) degree in computer science won't help these children sell more coconuts.

Someone else not going to school is the son of one of the captains of the other tourist sailboats. He takes his boy with him as he sails back and forth between Panama and Colombia. "My son's homeschooled," said the captain, when he earlier boarded our boat for a chat and a beer.

I said, "With sailing and looking after guests, how do you have time to do that?"

"Well, to be honest, he usually sort of homeschools himself."

Benny and Lucie and Sam and I play volleyball on the beach until we hear the sound of a conch blown, the signal that lunch is served: a barbecue on the beach. Slabs of pork and beef, a selection of sausages, salad on the side, spicy salsas. So much meat, too much to finish. (The sausages have hardly been touched, people put off by two gay dogs a metre away at it like viagra-charged gigolos.)

"I always cook too much," says Francia, "because I come from a large family. I'm the fourth of six siblings."

I ask how often she goes home.

"Not for two years."

Sam says, "We'll be eating this for days."

But we won't: "What we don't eat now we'll give to the Gunas," says Francia. "It's a nice treat for them: every day they have only seafood and coconuts."

As we're readying to leave Akuadargana, placing our trash in sacks to take back onto the boat, Francia nods at a girl next to a man who splits a coconut with a stroke of his machete. "You see her? She is a boy. This family had no daughters, so they raised their last boy as a girl. They dressed him as a girl and taught him to behave feminine. Sexually also he'll take the role of a female. This is common in Guna Yala, is one of their traditions." Other boys, I learn, choose to become *omeggid* — "like a woman". It's without stigma, perhaps because Guna Yala's society is matrilineal. Men move into the woman's family home, and household finances are in the hands of the wife, and work done by women — cooking, stitching, childcare — isn't thought lesser work. And the most important celebrations in Guna

Yala are a girl's birth, puberty, marriage. In such a place —
where, unlike almost everywhere else, society favours
women more than men — why would a bloke not want to
be a bird?

We sail on to Miriadiadup, part of the Cayos Holan-
deses, the islands furthest from the mainland. Miriadiadup
is smaller than Akuadargana, but otherwise similar: huts
and palms and mounds of coconuts. No omeggid but an
albino. Gunas, I'm told, have the highest occurrence of
albinism in the world: 1 in 150. Worldwide it's 1 in 20,000.
These so-called "Children of the Moon" have a duty only
they can do: on a lunar eclipse everyone but them must take
cover inside, while they go outside to shoot arrows at the
evil dragon that's eating the moon.

Jarri takes Lucie, Sam, and I out on the motor dinghy —
a bouncy, flimsy craft — and we zip about between deserted
islands where are not even footprints. Then we idle and chat
and swim, muse what a life it must be to live here, to live
lazy days in such sweet serene beauty. Might though, I
wonder, paradise become a prison after a while if you can't
come and go as you please? When it rains, when there are
week-long storms: what do they do then?

Francia says, "They just sit in their huts."

She says she once spent five days on one of these islands.
"After two days I was bored."

I ask Benny if he would stay on one for a year, without
leaving, for £100,000.

"No," he says. "It's a year of my life lost."

I up my offer of money I don't have to a quarter of a
million, and he's tempted.

He asks, "What would I have to eat?"

"Same as the locals: seafood and coconuts."

"I'm vegan; I don't eat seafood."

"Then I hope you really like coconuts."

Francia points at an island fifty metres away, one with only a palm and three shrubs, and says it's her favourite of all the islands. "So small, so beautiful." She says that before it was larger, but it's slowly shrinking, soon to be swallowed by the sea. All these low-lying islands will submerge as the water rises. Some are already reduced to sandbanks. Some have already disappeared.

"I like to go to that island to meditate," she says. "Naked, normally. Meditation is better if you're naked."

I suggest we go do some naked meditation, but she's not keen. So I swim across to the oasis alone, and loaf in the scrap of shade. Perfection. Absolute peace. All is right with the world. *My* world, anyway; *the* world is as ailed as ever. But here, on an island to myself, Trump and terrorism and Aston Villa's terrible results are off the radar. Travel — this type of travel, long-term and overland — isn't a vacation, and is often anything but relaxing, but a day like today, I admit, is cream, is cherries.

Tomorrow a return to shitcake: 48 hours non-stop sailing across open sea to Colombia. "We set sail at sunrise," Francia says, when we're back on the boat, "so start taking seasickness pills tonight."

SAN BLAS ISLANDS TO CARTAGENA

I sit cross-legged at the front of the boat. Silence but for the wind on the sails, the slight splash of waves. Since leaving paradise yesterday morning, we've seen nothing, zilch, nada. Not a single other ship in this watery desert between Panama and Colombia, between Americas central and south. So far from home, so far from anything, voyaging through a sea of thought, pondering existence: *What are we but specks of insignificance on the surface of this thing called earth?*

My meditations are splintered when I'm soaked by a rogue wave. "Sorry, man," comes a shout from the rear. "Didn't see it coming." Sam's at the wheel; one holds it, the other holds a beer. Captain Sam is a stopgap measure while Jarri — who takes two-hour sleep shifts with Luis — resizes and reangles the bulging sails that brisk the boat on. Later I'm in the hot seat: Jarri wants me to steer while he tinkers and tightens. At first I'm anxious — if we sink while I'm at the wheel, I'll feel guilty — but it's not long before I'm

loving the power. Perhaps I'll become a marauding bucca-
neer: sign-up with the Somalis, maybe, or go it alone on a
pedalo. Three-Willy Walters has a nice ring to it.

We walk like crabs, take slow steps sideways, and
Francia was right when she said, "Men, you need to sit to
pee. Welcome to our world." It gets messy if you stand. I've
had nine doses of Dramamine — the medication for
seasickness — and it's worked, I'm feeling alright. I'm not
even drowsy, as others are — a misspent youth, I guess. It's
KO'd Lilly; on her shelf-like bed, she looks like she's in a
coma. "People are like babies for this stage of the trip," says
Francia, nodding at Sarah and Lucie, curled up on the seats.
"All they do is sleep and eat." Eat cereal and toasted sand-
wiches, bowls of nuts and crisps; the food basic now we're at
sea. A cruise this isn't, and decorum we're without: Sam and
I are shirtless; everyone is barefoot; each of us stinks. Our
skin is salty, sticky, grimed. Five days without a shower.

Tiny to start with, the boat feels even smaller now that
we can't leave it to eat or walk or swim. Space and privacy
are at a premium and should have been even more pinched:
the ship has beds for ten guests, yet there are only six of us.
Normally, Francia says, there are ten.

I ask if she likes being out at sea. "It gets boring?"

Perched on a stool, sipping coffee-rum, she says, "I love
it: time for resting and reading and thinking. It's like hell for
some; they need to be busy, doing this or that. It's hard for
them to do nothing, and on here at sea that's all there is:
nothing."

Nothing but each other. After five days in each other's
faces we're strangers now friends. Lucky to have this easy-
going, low-key group; a loudmouth, a madman like

Thor, would be insufferable in these claustrophobic conditions where a fart in a cabin can be heard at the bow and smelt at the stern. Francia says the worst group they had was ten Aussies, all blokes: "They were drunk from the start of the first day to the end of the last."

Nature provides an occasional distraction: a lone bird, wings spread, gracefully gliding — the first sign of life since San Blas — and a pod of a dozen dolphins playfully diving in and out the water beside the boat. Off the rear reach a couple of fishing lines, but bugger all has bitten. Francia says it's a shame we haven't caught any white lobsters.

I've never heard of lobsters being white. "They're expensive because they're rare?"

She laughs. "White lobster is slang for cocaine chucked overboard by smugglers pursued by the police."

This is a prime spot for it: the start of the cocaine corridor that stretches from Colombia to the clubs of Miami. She says the coastguard or police often board the boat. "It can take three hours. They check every bag, every cupboard. They swab the surfaces, sometimes bring a dog on board. But never when we arrive in Cartagena, only when we leave there. No one smuggles cocaine into Colombia."

As the sun sinks in the burnt pink sky, land arises on the horizon: the north coast of Colombia, the twinkling orange lights of Cartagena. The black blurs of tankers and cargo ships slip by as we sail into the marina.

And so starts South America.

We drop our bags at hotels, then enter the UNESCO-listed 16th-century *Centro Historico*: Under the arch of the ornate yellow clocktower, the Puerta del Reloj, through the

Plaza de los Coches, where chained-up African slaves were once traded as if pigs; along narrow, curving cobbled streets, taking in the sights and sounds of this colonial treasure that flourished from the gold that flowed through from across the continent, from where set sail bullion-laden galleons bound for Madrid: The courtyards and fountains, the colourful mansions with flowering balconies; the sounds of salsa and guitars strummed in arcaded squares, the clip-clop of hooves drawing carriages; the door porn, the arches, the palms; the sense of Spain, of Italy; the citrus-coloured cathedral a stone's throw from the Palacio de la Inquisicion, where accused apostates were tortured; the statue of Simon Bolivar, saviour of South America; the lovers astride cannons atop the city walls; the sweeping views of the sea.

Then for ceviche and Aguila at La Vieja Guardia: a pretty place with pink walls and white wooden balconies. Ceviche finished, Francia, with a wink, hands me a tissue. I know what's within. Go to China, taste the noodles. Go to France, drink the wine. Go to Colombia, . . . The world's purest, the world's cheapest — £7 for this gram. And no need to fret about the feds: up to a gram isn't illegal in Colombia. No fine, no prison, no nothing.

"It's not like the coke in Europe," Francia whispers as I stand to go for a wee I don't need, "so don't do a line, just put some on the end of a key."

Into the toilet, open the tissue: there it is, sealed in a small baggie. Insert the key; key to nose; *snniiiffff*. Switches flipped: On, on, on; liftoff. I'm not a connoisseur of cocaine, but I know this is grade A candy. This stuff would make a gangster of Gandhi. I'm a Fiat Punto, usually; right now I'm a Ferrari. Give me a Sudoku; I'd solve it in seconds. An exam in Spanish: I'd ace it. I could run a marathon. I could cure cancer. I won't do any of those things, I'll just sniff, sniff, sniff, but I could, I damn well could.

From the old town to Getsemani, a former sketchy quarter and red-light district rehabbed: cutesy-coloured buildings garlanded with bougainvillea and hanging baskets, wooden-shutter windows wide open; lanes little larger than alleys suffused dim-orange, graffiti and murals on the walls; artists at easels, cool bars and cafes, stalls selling crepes and arepas. At its heart is Plaza de la Santisima Trinidad: a palm-lined square in front of a yellow-painted, centuries-old church. It's packed though it's only a Wednesday, buzzes with laughs and chatter; tourists and locals alike with glasses of Aguila in hand. Among the throngs are hawkers selling jewellery, tours, hats. Whatever they sell, "White coffee," is the whisper — caution because possession isn't illegal, but to sell it is. I wonder if coke is all that's sold, that all else is a front. Even Benny is asked — a guy with glasses and a bumbag, someone that makes librarians look like rockstars.

"What are you looking for?" says one man. "Somewhere to eat? A place to drink? White coffee?"

I have some of mine left, but why not? At this price it's as good as free. Francia by now has gone, and this guy is as good as any other. Except he's not: he sells me sugar and scarpers before I realise.

Sam points out a musician he spoke with: twenties, shades and a cool hat, carrying a guitar case. A safe bet. "I don't sell it, but I can get some for you," he tells me. "I'm a, how can I say, assistant to someone who sells it."

"How much?"

"£5."

I say I'll take two.

He says, "Wait a few minutes, and then we'll take a walk. A lot of police about."

It's true; it's crawling with cops clad in green, "POLICIA" printed on their caps and hi-vis vests. More pass through on motorcycles. A pair of suspect scallywags are pushed against a wall, aggressively searched.

Musician delivers. I stash one in a crack in the fan in my room. Then I go to Mamallena's for drinks and sniffs, by now past the key and on to lines. For a few hours: rah, rah, rah, go here, go there, laying tracks for the nasal train, spieling powder-powered monologues of nonsense. Flying, fucking flying, higher than I've flown before.

I'm back at my minuscule, barely-lit, musty room at 4am when I hear Sam return. "Sarah, Sarah, Sarah," he shouts, knocking on the door to their room. I open my door, ask him what's up.

"She has the only key to the room, and she must have passed out."

He comes into my room and we do some coke he has left. There's a fridge with beers in reception; we buy a couple, stand on the street outside the hotel to drink them. At this time all that remain are stragglers: a couple of arse-holed Argentinians chatting to some hussies outside the brothel next door — "Only £20," one tells us — and a trans-sexual flashing her boobs: "Nice, right? My cousin paid for them." A guy comes, a mini Mike Tyson, openly selling baggies. He tips one into the palm of his hand: "Go on, try it." Sam buries his nose into it, at it like a pig at a trough. He gets it all over his nose. "You look like a clown," laughs Mini

Mike. He walks off, chuckling to himself. "A fucking clown. Hahaha."

Another beer, another blast of coke. The next beer, the receptionist hesitates. He seems to think: *Is it wise to sell beer to this pair at 5am?* "Ok, guys," he says, "but keep it calm. I see you going in and out, in and out." He sniffs his nose, rolls back his eyes, waves his hands about — and I thought we were being discreet. "Only do it in the room, and be cool out on the street."

The sun rises as we drink the beer. Carts wheel along the street, coffee and breakfast for those who's day is set to begin as ours is due to end. For Sam it does — "Sarah will kill me unless I go to this mud-bath thing today." For me, not yet. Back in bed, I stare at the fan, think of the baggie within. *No*, I tell myself. *Save it.* And I do — for fifteen minutes.

I sit on the edge of the bed, hold up the baggie. *My precious.* I empty it over the ledge below the frosted window that looks onto the corridor. I chop it with a bank card, rack a long line, roll a note. *Snniiiffff.* I fall back onto the bed. The rush comes; rising, rising, rising. Sprawled and sighing with ecstasy, spells casting from my swirling fingers to the rhythms of The Stone Roses, David Bowie, Oasis. Rack. *Snniiiffff.* Because however high you are, one more line offers the promise of flying higher. Rack. *Snniiiffff.* Bringing my brain to orgasm — again and again and again. Rack. *Snniiiffff.* Sod San Blas and screw volcanoes; this is better than either. Rack. *Snniiiffff.* I'm the heavyweight champion of the world. Rack. *Snniiiffff.* The fucking resurrection.

"Yellow matter custard . . . Dripping from a dead dog's eye . . . ," I sing, hours later, sat on the shitter, forehead rested on the sink. "Crabalocker fishwife, pornographic priestess . . . Boy, you've been a naughty girl . . . You let your knickers down . . ." I get a whiff of the deposit; it smells like Chanel. "I am the egg man . . . They are the egg men . . . I am the walrus . . . Goo goo g'joob, goo goo goo g'joob . . . Goo goo g'joob, goo goo goo g'joob, goo goo." Washing my hands, I look in the cracked mirror; back at me looks reality. I recognise that face, that wild-eyed numbness, recognise it from last night, on the street, in the bars. I look like I've done a stint in Guantanamo Bay. But on I go: Rack. *Snniiiffff*. Rack. *Snniiiffff*. Rack. *Snniiiffff*. Blood begins to trickle from one nostril: a sign from my body telling me to stop. My body says no, but my mind says yes, oh yes. My mind says this is why we have not one but two nostrils; says Darwin probably — no, almost definitely — wrote a chapter about this in *On the Origin of Species*. Rack. *Snniiiffff*.

4pm now; still not asleep. I last did a line at 11am when the stash expired. Since then I've tried to sleep but have failed, and the devil is prodding flirtatiously, inviting me to dance: *Go out, pick up a fourth*. That, though, would be insane; if I continue, can I ever stop? I need to sleep; that will silence the temptation.

5pm, out on the streets, on the hunt for sniff. Sketchy and shaking, fretting my pupils will be reported as UFOs. No white coffee whispers; it's too early. I wander around, waiting for an offer. Then I spot a bloke opposite Mamallena's; he's stood by the window ledge of a boarded-up building, holding a tray of Trident and Marlboro. A flashback to last night: I was tipped off he sells. I walk over, stroke my chin. "How much are the cigarettes?"

"£3."

I wait a couple of seconds, seeing if he offers extras. He doesn't. I ask, "Do you have anything *else?*"

He pauses, looks me straight in the eye. "*Cocaina?*"

"Yeah."

"I have."

"How much?"

"£7."

I say I'll have one.

He says, "You want four? £20."

That would be ridiculous. "One is fine."

I hand over the cash. He looks about, then dips his hand into a bag; he pulls out something and puts it in my hand. I look at it: a lollipop. "What the—," I say, then I see what's under the lollipop.

Rack. *Snniiiffff.* I'd like to say the drugs don't work, they just make me worse. But one line and I'm as high as I was. I sniff until my other nostril goes on strike, then I'm reduced to rubbing it on my gums. All too soon that gram is gone. Desperate for scraps, I swipe a finger across the ledge. Below are my flip-flops; I spot a stray speck, dab it.

Wrapped in a sheet to protect myself from a mosquito I'm too ruined to pursue, I suck the lollipop and stare at the fan above whirring its rackety rounds, hoping it hypnotises me into sleep. Cocaine is energy on credit, to be paid back with interest — and the bailiffs arrive now and smash down the door. I start to drown in despair and paranoia, descend into the murky depths of my mind.

Psst. Psst. Psst: The devil whispers, says he has a solution.

If cocaine were legalised worldwide, civilisation would collapse. Children would starve as parents sniffed them-selves into comas. Because no amount is enough. You think:

A gram, that's plenty, probably even a bit left at the end of the night. Then there are just a few lines left. *I wish I had more, but no worries.* Then it's the last line. *Well, that's that.* Then you want more.

And to get more now is easy. From my room to get it and back to my room: three minutes. It would take longer to buy an aspirin.

Psst. Psst. Psst.

MEDELLIN

"People ask me, with a look of suspicion: 'Juan, it isn't the capital of Colombia, but it has the only metro in the country, and it's clean and modern and there's a lot of wealth around; where did the money to build Medellin come from?' In other words, they want to know if Medellin is a city built on drug money."

That's what I'm wondering, walking around downtown Medellin on this tour with Juan — fedora, red t-shirt, skinny jeans. Colombia's second city — a fourteen-hour bus ride south of Cartagena — is as he says: clean, modern, monied. Newly-minted high-rises bloom within the green slopes of the Aburra Valley. Districts like Poblado and Laureles are comfortingly middle-class. And where we are now, in businesslike Alpujarra, suits are suave and lattes are sipped.

Juan goes on: "The money from drugs came at the start of the 1980s. Medellin has been here much longer, hundreds of years. The money to build the city came from coffee and mining and textiles. This province, Antioquia, is Colombia's primary exporter, accounts for almost 15% of Colombia's GDP."

He admits that 2-3% of the GDP of Colombia comes from drugs. "That's billions of dollars," he says. "But that money does more harm than good. Fear. Blood. Suffering. That is what cocaine brings to the people of Colombia. There are no benefits: no improvements in infrastructure, healthcare, education. That money goes into the pockets of narcos. The majority of it to tax havens abroad."

Next to Alpujarra is Parque de las Luces: a glass-front library; 300 pillars that resemble lightsabers; ranks of blue bicycles with baskets (free to borrow). "This square and the surrounding neighbourhood were a no-go area until twenty years ago," says Juan. "The burnt-out market that was here was overtaken by criminals and the homeless. What we did here we have repeated at half a dozen other places in the city."

And he says 10,000 homeless twenty years ago are now 3,000. "Slowly, we're getting there."

Of the metro — propped on hulking concrete supports that run like a spine through the city — and the cable cars that rise out of it, Juan says they sewed Medellin together, connected downtown to the frayed, isolated outskirts. "It's more than a means of transport; it's a symbol of progress. Which is why people don't graffiti the metro, don't scratch the seats, don't leave trash on it."

He's right that they look after the metro. Despite being twenty-three years old, it looks like it's new.

A tsunami of people flood the grittier streets of down-town around San Antonio and Parque Berrio, where boxes and bags are carried on shoulders and wheeled along on carts, and hollering vendors peddle counterfeits and technicolour Saviours, watch-straps and superglue and porn. Flasks of coffee poured into plastic cups; fags sold in singles for a few hundred pesos each. Paninis not drugs being dealt; stacks of stickers in boxes, buyers flipping through. Other footie fans crowd in front of store windows to watch Munich v Madrid. A crowd also around an upturned cardboard box: one ball and three cups; bets are placed; no one wins. Red-lipped hookers in low-cut dresses propped against the white walls of Iglesia de la Veracruz, one of the city's oldest churches; they stroke their barely-covered bottoms and bounce their braless breasts as above them three bells toll atop the steeple. An Aldi of whores on the streets behind: the plump, the elderly, the addicted. Cheeks too pink and eyelids too blue; more silicon than San Francisco, more camel toes than the Sahara. They tap on phones, tap up passing perverts. Prey on the hook they slink up stairwells to the upper-floors of run-down buildings. Pimps skulk near, shifty in caps and trackies, hawk-like eyes on their slaves; some hand out flyers with photos and phone numbers — the women on the flyers look a species apart from those in the street. "It's not illegal in Colombia, but it's also not regulated by the government," says Juan. "£5 for one hour. Half goes to the girl, half to the pimp."

More booty and boobs in Plaza Botero — willies as well: twenty-three bronze statues by Medellin's golden child Fernando Botero. Half are naked fatties. One's a woman without a head or hands, but with finely-crafted knockers and punani. If *I'd* made a piece like that in art class, I'd have gotten an F and had my parents called in. Yet *he's* one of the most expensive artists alive; his sculptures sell for millions.

From there to Parque Bolívar — children playing and old fellas reading *El Colombiano;* a gaggle of transsexuals, suspiciously curvaceous; tramps and winos and a guy with eyes glazed, grinning and gibbering, holding a yellow bottle of glue. Then to Parque San Antonio, where in 1995 a bomb hidden in a statue killed dozens. Juan says, "Right-wing paramilitaries said it was them. Leftist guerrillas said it was them. Narcos said it was them. It was as if they were proud of the bomb."

In a Q&A Juan dismisses the Netflix show *Narcos* — "Only 10% of the story in that show is true." — and says it glamourises what was a hellish period. "Medellín was a war zone. Between 1983 and 1993, 37,000 were murdered."

He tells us that in the nineties two of his uncles were kidnapped. "For a year they were held in the jungle in a dungeon. To free them, my family paid a ransom: $500,000."

And he says: "When I was fifteen, playing football in the street with my friends, men on motorcycles came with Uzis. I was shot twice." He points to his leg and his arm. "Four of my friends were killed."

The main man — who he's been calling the "famous criminal" because he says many locals will be angry if they hear him or us use his real name — what of him?

Juan says, "Some say he killed a lot of people, but he also gave money to the poor and built them houses, so maybe he wasn't so terrible. To them I say, 'If he killed your child, your sibling, your parent: how many houses would he need to build to make up for it?' He was no hero, no Robin Hood. He was a terrorist and a paedophile."

A Dutch bloke isn't put off, asks about the tours centred

on the famous criminal: "Is it true we can meet his brother Roberto?"

Juan is enraged: "If you want to take one of those tours, look it up online. But let me ask: I was shot, my brother was shot, people close to me died, and you want to see where the guy to blame lived and meet his fucking brother?!"

A second tour in the afternoon. This one led by Dio, a uni student born and raised in Medellin. We get off the metro in the north of the city at a neighbourhood (*barrio* in Spanish) called Moravia. Home to 64,000, it's the highest density barrio in Colombia. Dio says, "Take a look at that hill; the nice one with the gardens." We look. It could be an allotment: plots of greens, yellows, and purples; blooming flowerbeds bordered by trimmed hedges. "This hill you see, it's not natural; it's a hill-sized pile of garbage. Dig down not even one metre and you'll find trash. Fifteen years ago it was a shantytown covered top to bottom in shacks. 8000 people lived on this steaming mound of rubbish."

In the fifties, he explains, refugees from conflicts in the countryside fled to cities that were full. They set up camp on the unused space on the outskirts. The settlements were illegal, but at the time they were out of the way, so the authorities largely let them be. By the seventies Moravia was full, but still people came, settling on the only ground that remained: the city dump. And there they stayed for thirty years. Dio says, "In 2004, under public pressure, the authorities finally built apartments for the people living on the hill of trash."

Then why are there still people living on the hill? 800 remain, living in homes that are dire. They're buildings but barely; it's scraping the barrel of the definition. Lopsided, misshapen, combustible. Pieced together and patched up with bricks, concrete, cinder blocks — so far, so good — advertising hoardings, scrap metal, cardboard, plywood, awnings, tyres, and all sorts of odds and ends. I look at a pile of trash outside one and wonder if it's for the binman or an extension.

Dio points at some grey blocks, hard to see in the distance: "Those are the apartments." The problem, he says, is that not only are they far from downtown where people make their living selling from carts and stalls but that there they have to pay taxes and bills; here, they don't. And for people employed informally, without a contract, cash in hand — as 50% of Colombians are — paying taxes and bills out of their £7-a-day salary is a stretch.

We circle the hill to enter the barrio; this part is flat and not built on trash. On lanes and alleys laid out like a maze are three-storey helter-skelter houses. Crudely constructed, cement clumsily applied with haste not care by builders drinking tequila not tea. Second floors poke over the first, third floors over the second; each a little wider to gain a little more space; the effect being reverse pyramids. To save space, stairs often outside rather than in; some to storeys not yet built, where rusted rods poke up and sacks of cement and stacks of bricks are piled. Laundry dries on hangers hung from chaotic, tangled cabling spread like silly string. Dogs snarl and vigilant heads peek out from upper floors and elderly women clutch barred doors as if they're in a cell. Colour is splashed with murals and mosaics — a boy pointing to the distance, expression of determination; a girl speaking into a megaphone — and the beehive buzzes with commerce: pharmacies and pet stores, bakeries and toy shops. When past us rides a motorcycle with a washing machine hitched to its rear, Dio says, "That guy takes his washing machine all over the barrio; he charges £1.50 for three hours use of it."

I ask, "Just that one guy? For 64,000 people?"

"Yes. But his business has grown; now he has three washing machines."

As for the people, they're friendly. "*Hola,*" say some. Others: "*Bienvenidos.*" Kids kicking a ball come over and speak a few words of English. I ask Dio if they think it's weird that we're here.

He says, "They're proud of their barrio and happy that you're here. For a long time no one could come. Then no one would come. You represent the progress they've made."

Because not long ago, for a foreigner to be here — any face unfamiliar — would be unthinkable. Even the police kept away. Dio says, "If cops tried to enter this barrio, people threw rocks at them." Hostility to officialdom also explains the seeming lack of logic to the layout. "They laid it out like this on purpose as a defence against the authorities, who sometimes tried to tear down parts of the barrio, which at that time was illegal."

It remained illegal until 1991 when Colombia introduced a new constitution. Dio says, "Because of that constitution, barrios built without permission became legal. The government recognised the people as the owners of the land and invested in infrastructure."

He credits the change of constitution for the decline in Medellin's murder rate, more so than the death of Voldemort — as Dio calls him. He shows us a graph: there's a distinct decline from 1993 — the year that Voldemort died

— but the drop starts in 1991. A second graph compares the murder rate in Medellin from 1975-2015 to that of Caracas in Venezuela (the most dangerous city in the world today). In 2015, Caracas reported 120 homicides per 100,000 people. Medellin peaked at 375 per 100,000: that's 6,000 murders in a year. In London last year: 116.

When Moravia was legalised, the authorities said its inhabitants could acquire ownership of their land by working for it. For the work they had to build the barrio, which at that point was a shantytown. They built the houses and paved the streets, laid pipes for plumbing and put up cables for electricity. "That's why everything looks kind of amateur," says Dio, "because they did it themselves." Now there's a medical centre providing subsidised healthcare, a community centre for kids and adults to take classes, a place for the elderly to get free meals. And schools — also free, which not all were until 2012.

"And this?" I ask, referring to an astroturf football pitch. "They built this too?"

"No. Voldemort paid for that. He came to barrios like this and built things. And he'd knock on doors to hand out cash: 'Hey, here's a thousand dollars.'"

Pocket change for a bloke that Forbes named in 1989 as the seventh richest in the world.

I ask, "So this barrio, they like Voldemort?"

"Here he's very, very popular."

There's been no sight of trouble, nor sense of it; at the end of the tour I ask if the barrio is as safe as it feels.

Dio says, "You don't see guns in the street or drugs dealt on corners because now the gangs are discreet."

"But the guns and drugs are still here?"

"Yes."

He says this is the case across Medellin and puts the relative peace down to pacts the gangs have with the authorities: to overlook criminal activities provided a sense of safety and order is maintained.

Violence erupts when those pacts break down. Like it has now in Comuna 13, the district beside Comuna 2 which houses Moravia (a *comuna* being a collection of neighbourhoods). Retaliating to weapons being seized — including grenade launchers — and the arrests of bosses, gangs have sparked a wildfire of terror. Buses have stopped serving parts of the district after one was torched and drivers were threatened. One of the metro-cable lines was temporarily suspended because passengers came under fire. And there have been several murders. So the district has been militarised. I see hardcore soldiers armed with assault rifles on patrol, and police stopping vehicles, searching and questioning, as I soar over the barrios of Comuna 13 cocooned in a perspex booth that glides up the valley to the elevated fringes of the city. Below is a blanket of bricks stitched with snaking alleys. Looked at from downtown, these homes merge into a mass, appear as if a single structure, a fortress spanning the slopes. Up close they're a rank smear of red-brick syphilis.

Comuna 13 is the poster child for the metamorphosis of Medellin; that, though, is a misrepresentation, is only La Independencia — one strip of one barrio of twenty-three in Comuna 13. Earlier I visited: funky-coloured houses and zigzagging orange-roofed escalators; somersaulting break-dancers and inspired, artistic murals and stores selling t-shirts; a one-legged pensioner in a wheelchair looking curiously at tourists licking mango lollies. Search "Comuna 13" on Google Images and that's what you'll see: a veneer in a mouth of septic teeth.

For all the talk of "transformation" — a word used to exhaustion in reference to Medellin — the truth is that swathes of it are still off-limits: sloppily-built, labyrinthine, favela-style barrios. It's a city rising and rebranded; happily-ever-after, though? No. Fifty-plus murders this month; nearly two hundred this year so far (it's only April; a 24% rise on last year). And armed robberies have tripled in recent years. But in what was hell there is hope. And for now that will do.

JARDIN TO QUITO

Mist rises like smoke from forest that climbs to the peaks of this verdant crease of the Andes. The Cristo Rey — a toy-town Christ the Redeemer — like a Christmas tree decoration atop a point of green, surveys glossy coffee plants and large-leafed banana groves and sleepy streets of floral, quaint homes with shutters pulled back — within are solemn statues of saints and portraits of ancestors, crockery in cabinets and silverware and stiff sofas. As well as homes, one-room workshops where shirts are sewn and doors are sanded and engines are greased. And muddied veteran jeeps and workers in wellies with sacks heaved over shoulders. In the pastel-splashed Parque el Libertador, beds of roses — red, pink, and white — and aged trees and spruced hedges and ornate lampposts. Jets of water from a fountain; in jumps a Labrador. Stalls sell pears and grapes and carrots and parsnips; from one the smell of buttery popcorn. At tables apt for a tea party with the Mad Hatter, people sip *cafe tinto* or coffee with a kick: a drop of brandy, of Amaretto.

A portly fellow snores; in front of him a table of empty glasses. Other locals lost in talk or sat alone smiling or bobbing their head to a folk song: the bald, blind player croons; his fingers silkily coast along the keys of his accordion. Ponchos and fedoras, check shirts and Stetsons. Moustaches are in fashion. Dominos placed and cards played; hands move pawns and rooks. Grain is thrown to pigeons and toddlers chase after them; a boy catches one, parades it like it's the FA Cup, kissing it's head and holding it aloft.

On one side of the *parque* is the twin-spired neo-gothic-style Basilica Menor de la Inmaculada Concepcion. A church fit for Vienna. It towers over the town, a constant reminder that He is always watching. And if you can't see it, you can hear it: the bells toll every fifteen minutes, setting the rhythm of the day. Worshippers in, out, in, out of the high-arched entrances, doing a religious hokey-cokey. Melodic hymns from within, where are columns and confession booths and scenes of the crucifixion. At the front a grandiose marble altar, yellow flowers in lavish vases, statues of praying angels. Choir boys in red flank a priest robed in silky white; he sing-songs verses, reaches a crescendo. "Amen," from the congregation crammed snugly onto pews too few. Some stand at the back, the sides; some have brought their own chair. Had I been born here in Jardin, a contradiction to the consensus of Colombia as a country of cocaine, conflict, chaos, I too may have believed.

Stay I could, retire, idle, age, but on I must move. I've been too much of a tourist, travelling only in bursts. Six months since Los Angeles, I could have reached Rio de Janeiro in three. Now I'll roll and roll along rivers and roads — the first this snaky road out of town: pocked with brown puddles, spattered with stinking manure, past trout farms and rusty-roofed farmhouses, through pastures studded with wildflowers where mares drink from streams and stocky cattle graze. Then a curvy ascent on what feels like a backroad to Heaven: wildly wooded, torrenting waterfalls, glistening and haunting and opaque; a sense of Middle-Earth, a setting for dwarves and dragons. Branches brush the windows as we labour up rough slivers of road little wider than the bus. None of it's paved; rocks litter it from roadside rockfaces part-collapsed. Barriers, where there are any, are barbed wire, half a metre: that's all between us and a vertiginous plummet. As battered a bus as I've seen, it isn't fit for the job. Windscreen cracked; taped wires hang. Soil and grass and leaves on the seats, a third of which are broken. It sways and groans and rattles, shakes my organs, my bones. Several times I'm flung from my seat. Astronauts could be trained on here. No matter how buggered a bus is, the speakers always work — chirpy, vocal salsa today. Another axiom of travel to be relied upon: the more shite a bus is, the more religious images and idols there are. This bus could be a gift store at the Vatican.

Half an hour in we jerk to a halt. Forwards, backwards, forwards, backwards. A problem. The driver dressed in double denim gets off, is on his hands and knees to inspect under the bus. In and out three times in five minutes; hands on hips, grimacing. Out come a toolbox and a pack of fags. With a wrench and a cigarette, anything can be fixed. We all get off the bus; in the road, waiting and watching. No one moans. Buses like this, roads like this: it's par for the course. The driver jacks the bus, then lays beneath grunting and panting, cigarette jutting from his mouth. CRASH. Down slams the bus. We all flinch but not the driver. He takes a pull on his fag, then starts to again jack the bus. He stands after fifteen minutes; he strokes his chin then shrugs his shoulders and tells us to get back on board. He's a believer; on his neck hangs a cross. I prefer a driver to be an atheist: a religious driver cares little about death because he thinks Heaven awaits. With the steering screwed and hours to go on circuitous mountain passes, I consider walking back to Jardin. But I don't. The odds of dying have risen from 0.01% to 5%. Still good odds.

Minutes later: *screeeechhh*. The road is blocked with rubble fallen from a five-storey rockface. We file off the bus and set to work to shift the rocks — at it like a chain gang at a gulag. Some are minor boulders, require multiple hands to move. The driver uses the time to ride back and forth over a rock he's placed behind a front tyre. The engine grinds, the chassis clunks. Someone asks what he's doing. He grabs his shoulder and motions pushing it into position, like a doctor rectifying a dislocated shoulder. We drive on — in a place with no AA that's what you do until the engine explodes or the wheels fall off. The odds of death have risen to 8%. More people die on buses like this on roads like this than die skydiving or bungee jumping. But I like these roads, these buses. The bus from Cartagena to Medellin was one of the best I've ever been on: back-of-seat screens, wifi that worked, clean toilets. Of that trip I remember nothing — I may as well have been on a plane. This, though — this today, this road, this bus — is travel in the truest sense. I'll stay on board until the odds of death are 51%.

We pit stop on a peak by a rickety ramshackle restaurant. A pig outside snuffles in thicket beside a bamboo crucifix that slants over a misty gorge. While the driver again rides to and fro over a rock, crisps and biscuits are bought from a waddling, gummy woman, and coffees are sipped from chipped china bowls. A French woman is hit on by my seatmate — a man of forty with a moustache and curly black locks. He has no luggage but a toothbrush, which pokes from the pocket of his oversized leather jacket. His eyes are bloodshot; he yawns repeatedly. Still pissed, probably, because she resembles The Scream. She comes to me: "Can I stand with you? That guy's talking about him and me getting married."

On we ride into alpine meadows; soaring, skinny trees and dilapidated homesteads. A ghostly whiteness dissolves buildings to traced outlines, people to spectral sketches. Then a winding descent to shabby Rio Sucio. The bus station is a shipping container in the car park of a football stadium. There I change to a minivan, set off for Pereira. A curl down to the crumpled valley floor, scenes similar to those around Jardin. We then flank the Rio Cauca, brown and twisting, through grasslands and orchards, and cruise through undulating Constable-like countryside. Into Eje Cafetero — fertile Andean foothills that are thick with coffee bushes dripping with raindrops. Colombia is the world's third largest exporter. It produces 810,000 tons of coffee. Cocaine? 1,500 tons. Yet the notion persists that it's a one-crop country. Most of its coffee is grown on small family *fincas* like these beyond the window. Handpicked — the terrain, angled at 55-plus degrees, precludes machinery — by some of the half a million Colombians that earn their crust from coffee. Through Manizales, a miniature Medellin and the region's coffee HQ, and along a smooth highway through sprawling bottle-green plantations, over a ridge and around a hairpin into Pereira: low-rise but sprouting.

Bus stations are never buildings of beauty as train stations can be. Modern is the best you can hope for. Safe will do. This one has the look of an eighties shopping centre in Stoke. Tubed lights, brightness set to bleak. A rabbling, muffled tannoy that sounds more like Arabic than Spanish, and LEDs flashing places I've never heard of: Ibague, Mocoa, Buga. Dumpy, grumpy women at ticket booths. Pot-bellied drivers that are photofits of paedophiles; their shoes too shiny, their short-sleeved shirts two sizes too large. Rows of stiff metal chairs; a man that smells of boiled cabbage sitting beside me despite half the seats being empty. The Discovery Channel without sound: a guy tries to haul a fish the size of a shark into a boat the size of a bath. A sparsely-stocked pharmacy and a cafeteria displaying faded, low-def photos of sorry-looking frankfurter hotdogs. Sad meals of sweaty chicken and microwaved *bunuelos*. Instant coffee. I pay to take a dump; I pay extra for bog roll (she gives me three sheets); I waste a sheet to wipe pubes and piss off the seat. I psychoanalyse a stranger based on the way they walk and the brand of their luggage: I conclude there's no hope for them and they should be euthanised. I question my sanity; I reassure myself that I know at least half a dozen people more mental than me and that I'm safe until they start being sectioned; I make a note of their names and addresses to give the men in white coats in case they come for me first.

Out of Pereira towards Salento on lanes through swells of hills. A lead sky. A brisk breeze smelling of spring. Cows and pastures, rose bushes along the central reservation. It could be England, the Malverns or Staffordshire. Sweet scenes graffitied with grating sounds. Israelis arguing. A woman playing a game on an iPad: *Ting. Ting-ting. Ting-ding-ta-da.* Another woman listens to Christian ballads on her phone. She sings along. If she's going to Heaven, I'm glad I'm set for Hell. On the road I let things slide, I don't speak up. It's their house, their rules. In the UK I'm not so passive; I let rip if someone's being a social retard. Some poor sod will get it big time when I'm back, will feel the force of months of pent-up wrath. He'll be on the X2 bus to Brum and open a pack of crisps, and I'll go postal on him. "You noisy, selfish bastard," I'll yell as I smash his face against the window. "Enjoy eating your Wotsits without any teeth, you fucking wanker."

Hairpin bends up a hillside to Salento: a plaza and a church, candy-coloured houses with clay-tile roofs. A pretty place but in *the book*. Sold its soul, tailored itself for tourist dollars. I've soon snubbed Salento and am on a bus on the highway to Armenia, then onwards to Ibague: rising into the Andes, a crawl up switchbacks and hairpins slicked by showers. Peaks and gorges, green and mist. Humble abodes tacked on angular contours. People scarce: a bent back at work with an axe, a wanderer in wellies with a mule. Then an eel-like descent through mountain woodlands into the Quindio Pass through which we twist and bend. Steep sides of deep greens, peaks and ledges and cliffs. High up them, on gradients gravity-defying, huts and houses seemingly magnetised. Others are propped over ravines by rotting wooden scaffolding. We trail a river through tropical forest where grows guava and papaya and bananas, through Caja-marca, through Cocora, through Ibague. Out then of the

Andes, belting along a rural road to Neiva. A yellowing of the landscape; some cacti, then a rocky desert. We skirt the desert and the land livens en route to Pitalito. Squat, sleepy pueblos slip by, scarcely distinguishable. Always a church, always a plaza.

The change to note is the checkpoints. From none to few in the north and Eje Cafetero, they're staged at frequent intervals. Mexico's Baja California was the entrance to the destination; here is the exit from the source. This road is a corridor through coca-growing hotspots. The province of Cauca — 50 km west of here, and this road later cuts into its southern reaches — produces more than anywhere else in Colombia. And east of here is the Amazon, which covers a third of the country; coca grown there and processed into powder in low-key labs on its fringes is trafficked through here to the Pacific. A quarter of a century since You-Know-Who was gunned down on a Medellin rooftop, Colombia remains the world's largest producer. Production was at a record high in 2017. Try as they might — and they have, with both carrot and stick strategies: manual uprooting and aerial fumigation; paying farmers to change crops — the Colombian government is impotent. In late 2016 they even made peace with FARC — the Marxist guerrillas whose nefarious tentacles had a stranglehold on swathes of the country, and whose narco-dollar militia were as well-armed as the army. FARC controlled two-thirds of the coca crops in the country, but as they withdraw, others move in. Much to the annoyance of America, who since 2000 have given Colombia billions of dollars in aid for the war on drugs. A war sure to be lost because cocaine is better than sex and the cash to be made is crazy. *The Guardian* reported that a kilo of cocaine in the Colombian jungle sells for $3,000. Once into the US it sells for $35,000 wholesale and on the street for more than $100,000.

Checkpoints are sometimes the police, other times the army. Police, it's often a pair: motorcycles roadside, a few cones set up. Army: sandbag bunkers beside dark-green vehicles topped with heavy guns. The soldiers are baby-faced, fresh out of boot camp. They look to be kids playing dress-up. But their chunky, black guns look real. At each checkpoint a quarter of vehicles are stopped and searched. Details of IDs are noted, radioed through; some people are photographed. At one an officer steps into the road and faces his palm at our van. The officer slides open the door, asks for IDs. Satisfied that none of us are wrong 'uns, he sends us on our way. Twice more we're stopped, the third instance resulting in a 15-minute search of the van. Scant chance of finding anything: it would be foolish to use a road like this to traffic drugs when there are plenty of other routes. They're effectively ornaments, these soldiers, these police. The flow of cocaine is unstoppable; they merely redirect it elsewhere.

From Pitalito to Mocoa we drive beside Colombia's oldest national park — the Parque Nacional Cueva de los Guacharos. Then we recross the Andes, circularly climbing a narrow gravel road, the scenes like those from Jardin to Rio Sucio, from Armenia to Ibague. All but a metre ahead is veiled white by formless vapour that absorbs the daylight, the ravines, the peaks, the road; at times even that metre ahead ceases, and it's as if we're in flight through nothing-ness, in a wormhole to another dimension. Signs prep the driver: right turn, hard left, hairpin. Some say simply

"*Peligro*" (Danger). We negotiate streams across the road that cascade over the precipice, and edge by workers repairing wrecked barriers, and pass sentries stationed in pillboxes — barrels peeped through loopholes. As we curl back down along a road scratched on the mountainside, and the shroud of vapour subsides, woodland engulfs the slopes: blankets of broccoli spread over a battalion of sleeping giants. I'm a child on Christmas morning, but others sleep — the bounce of the wheels making their heads loll like rag-dolls. Not a trace of excitement in those awake; not one looks out the window. They've seen it before; they're locals. Since Armenia, no foreigners.

Through Sibundoy and past Laguna de la Cocha, then via Pasto to Ipiales, hurtling along the Pan-American Highway through patchworks of pastures and fields of crops knitted with hedges. At Ipiales is a yellow bridge — the *Puente Internacional Rumichaca* — that connects Colombia and Ecuador. Horns blare from taxis and minivans, grubby fingers thumb wads of notes as thick as bricks, and confused people wander to and fro, wonder where to go, what to do — I'm one of them. It should be simple: exit stamp from Colombia; then entry stamp for Ecuador. Complicating the situation is a five-wide queue outside the Colombian immigration building, stretching fifty metres from the entrance, then 360 degrees around. Nearly a thousand people. I walk twice around the gated red-brick building, hoping that I've missed something, that it's the wrong queue. But it's not. I join it. To pass some time I work out how long I'll be in the line. If it takes three minutes to process each person: a day and a half.

I see a pair of lanky blokes — one bald, one with his

blonde hair in a bun — wearing luminous-yellow water-proof overalls, of the type worn by fishermen. They're by the entry gate in a group that isn't part of the queue. I ask them what's going on.

Baldie says, "They're refugees from Venezuela, heading south to Ecuador and other countries."

I look at the queue; before I saw them as one mass, ignored the details; now I see shaggy suitcases, carts of belongings, gallon bottles of water, duvets and pillows, wailing babies, wheelchairs. One man has a pile of five and ten cent coins. He carefully counts them: "... *un dollar* ... *cinco, quince, viente* ... *dos dollar* ... *diez, viente, trente* ..."

"I think we won't have to join the queue," says Man Bun. "I feel bad about it, but it's not the blue-eyed privilege. We have passports; they haven't."

He's right: some have slips of paper, others sheaves of documents.

Man Bun speaks to the guard, points at his mate and me. The guard opens the gate; we slip inside. I feel the stares, sense the hundreds of head-shakes at the fishermen and their friend. They think we're dicks. I think so too.

A second queue inside. While waiting, Man Bun and Baldie tell me they're motorcycling through South America.

"For charity?" I ask.

"Just for fun," says Baldie.

"So why are you dressed as fishermen?"

He laughs. "They're overalls to keep our clothes clean and dry."

It takes an hour to get our exit stamps. While we've been inside only a couple of dozen of the masses outside have been let in. We exit past the weary people with their bags and bundles, walk under a sign — *"Gracias por visitar la Republica Colombia"* — and over the bridge to another: *"Bienvenido a la Republica de Ecuador"*. Another immigration building, another queue — long and wide, bent around the building, numbering a few hundred. We go to the front; within a minute we're inside. At the counter the officer asks no questions, stamps me into Ecuador. I've saved myself two days of queuing but have given up the right to ever complain about anyone queue jumping. A fair deal.

On the bus to Quito it's me and refugees. We're stopped at a checkpoint not far from the border. A police officer boards and asks for *documentos*. Palpable anxiety as he moves along the aisle inspecting and questioning. It takes an hour. When we're again in motion, high fives and fist bumps and whoops, and the white glare of screens as they sign in to Whatsapp and Facebook. *He can't be a refugee; he has a bloody phone*: the argument of the ignorant. But these people had to leave Venezuela. The country is imploding. I can't ask the escapees for the latest because — aside from my terrible Spanish — *Fast & Furious* plays on a TV at ear-abuse volume. Instead I search online. A *Washington Post* article from today titled "Venezuela deteriorates: Blackouts, hyperinflation, hunger":

"In the past 12 months the economy, public services, security and health care have all but collapsed . . . Militias are terrorizing urban areas, while police stand accused of extrajudicial killings . . . Four of the ten most dangerous cities in the world are now in Venezuela . . . Diseases once thought largely eradicated — malaria, diphtheria, measles and tuberculosis — are not only resurfacing but surging . .

. Schools are without teachers, hospitals are without doctors and nurses . . . The currency is so worthless that you could wallpaper a building with bills for less than the cost of paint."

So here they are with me on this bus, on the run: them from a repressive regime, a ruined state; me from routine and responsibility.

QUITO TO PANTOJA

Against a volcanic backdrop, a UNESCO-listed 17th-century colonial centre that's a catalog of grandeur: churches and fountains and columns and statues and plazas. Beyond that centre it's tatty; is grey lego strewn in a tantrum. Dreary in weather as well as character. *Ecuador* is Spanish for equator and Quito is almost bang on zero degrees latitude; altitude, though, messes with its weather: at 2850 metres, it's the second-highest capital in the world after La Paz in Bolivia. I wear three layers yet still feel the cold. So I'll skip through Quito. And largely through Ecuador. I only came because south-east Colombia — the most direct route to Peru — is a no-go zone. Ecuador is one of those countries that doesn't sound sexy. Paraguay, Belgium, and Canada are some others. About them I know little or nothing, but I've written them off. Whereas others about which I'm ignorant I've classed as must-sees: Iran, Kenya, Ethiopia, Kyrgyzstan, Madagascar. Discrimination rooted in what I don't know. I'll bus east across Ecuador to Coca, the entry to the Amazon;

then boat through Peru and into Brazil, go balls deep into the depths of the jungle. With a stop-off at Iquitos — a place that no roads go to or from — to drink ayahuasca, a brew sacred to the tribespeople of the Amazon — and the most powerful hallucinogenic known to man. I've met no one who's taken this route, no one who said they plan to. If shit's going wrong, it's this stretch that it will happen.

A well-paved highway out of Quito through an unremarkable landscape: hilly fields and rocky scrub and misty moors. The sky spits, the window steams. From the headrest, a stale, sicky stench stewed from thousands of heads. Screens unfold and a movie starts: soldiers shooting at aliens in a swamp. Volume too loud to ignore. The seat in front is reclined — the bastard is practically horizontal — and the bloke behind bashes my seat as if he's masturbating enthusiastically. The man beside leaks noise; he sniffs and snores and his phone beeps. Even his breathing is annoying — I wish he'd stop. He's also man-spreading, legs apart like he's riding a horse not sat on a bus. I want to punch his balls to teach him a lesson. But it's a long ride to Coca, and a long ride sat next to a man you've hit in the bollocks is awkward. I'll wait until we're five minutes from Coca. I can cope with five minutes of awkwardness.

I can't sleep so I try to watch the movie but it's awful — King Kong's fighting John Goodman. (Films on buses are the lowest common denominator, typically starring The Rock.) I listen to music; then change to an audiobook. But I can't concentrate. My mind wanders. I fidget. The window turns into a mirror, reflects rumbling ruminations. I rue mistakes and mull regrets — things done, things not done — and regurgitate unresolved grievances from the nineties, and recall every time I've been wronged, and relive shameful episodes, and repent my sins. Travel isn't an escape, as some say. Your troubles and sadnesses come with you as if packed in a suitcase. You can flee your job, your bills, your spouse. But you can't escape yourself. You're right there with you for the long haul. Neither is travel the way to "find yourself". If you want to do that, stare at a wall for a week — fewer distractions: volcanoes, cocaine, etc.

The start of every journey is always the same: a restless struggle. It's as if my mind is a child; as if I've brought on board a snotty brat. But it passes; it always passes. I soothe the child to sleep. Or strangle it to death. By the time The Rock is running along a beach in Speedos, the struggle has subsided, I've relaxed. I look at the time and think, Wow, four hours; if I've done four, I can do all day — watch the whole of The Rock's back catalogue. And not merely endure but enjoy the ride, relish the excused idleness. Because nothing's expected of the traveller. His hours are his own to while away as he wishes, need never be justified nor explained. The days are his. The weeks are his. The months are his. And if he is asked, and an answer is expected, the beauty is that being abroad classes as something even when most of the time there he does little.

A friend might ask, "What are you up to?"

"I'm in Ecuador."

"Cool!"

They said *what* not *where*, but they accept the where as a what.

We drive through the glistening greenness of the foothills of the Andes: low-hung clouds nestle over boggy earth; cattle graze by gushing streams; fifty-metre waterfalls cascade. Then a break at a bamboo-and-thatch restaurant where a snoozing Rottweiler opens a lazy eye and a girl in yellow wellies swings in a hammock. Stodge is spooned onto plates. "*No, gracias.*" On days I travel I never eat at roadside restaurants. A meal that at best is 3/10 at the risk of raping my bowels. Better to make do with candy. Tooth decay, yes; shitting my pants on a bus, no. So I buy a pack of Halls and for half an hour — until the eaters file out, toothpicks in mouths, waddling with post-stodge stupor — I walk loops of the car park and windmill my arms and crack my fingers. Breaks on buses are the only times I exercise.

We skirt the Cayambe Coca Ecological Reserve; from there into wet-and-wild woodlands, then remote highlands where are scrappy houses strung in twos or threes, an occasional featureless settlement straddling the road. The Rock is back — *Jumanji* — as we motor through Lumbaqui and Lago Agrio. By now away from the Andes, the land is flat and flush with cacao, bananas, coconuts. Then through Sacha and into Coca, where is a leafy brick-paved promenade parallel to a fast-flowing mud-brown river: the Rio Napo. Born from the slopes of Andean volcanoes, the Napo is a tributary of the Amazon and my route into the rainforest. I'll ride it for 900 kilometres to Iquitos; there it converges with its big bro. Though a tributary, the Napo is a beast. In Coca it's 200-or-so metres wide. But this is a thin section: its average width is more than a kilometre.

Slouched bodies and bored faces at the jetty on the promenade. All locals; for them it's a commute. Sacks and bundles stacked at the front of the long, thin boat: a sixty-seater with twin motors at the rear; so low sided as to be able to reach down and touch the river. Transporte Fluvial

Kamu Kamu #4 is its name. What happened to the first three? I wonder pessimistically. Beside the gangplank are a couple of stocky soldiers. One asks for my passport, asks where I'm going. No why; never a why; never a *Why the fuck are you here and not in an office updating a spreadsheet?* I take a seat on the boat. A man boards selling yoghurt; I decline: no one will take me seriously as a commando if I'm eating yoghurt. The Jabba in front eats one, then tosses the trash into the river. A toddler pisses off the side, his shirt gripped from behind by his father, and a mum waps out a tit for a baby that cries. The guy next to me says he's going to Peru to sell t-shirts. A long way to go to sell t-shirts, and he has no t-shirts with him, so that's likely not what he said. *Mi español es stillo shito.*

As coca recedes into the distance, leaden clouds spunk their load. Through a five-storey gauntlet of dense green — tree next to tree next to tree, vines on vines on vines — the Napo slithers like a vicious brown snake. It's littered with logs and branches, soon widens to at least a kilometre. We skim along one side, then slide to the other, back and forth, zigzagging, and arc around mid-river islands. Several times the engine cuts out and for a few seconds we drift. On the river barely a boat but ours: a few canoes, an occasional flat-deck barge loaded with tankers — "*Petroamazonas. Inflamable. Peligro.*"

Though not the Amazon River, this is the Amazon Rainforest: a region that's twice the size of India, that spans 40% of South America. 390 billion trees — that's not a typo: *billion*. And in one hectare of the Yasuni Reserve — that we flank for a while — is a wider variety of trees and birds and reptiles and amphibians than in all of the US. The most alive place on the planet, yet eerily silent and still. Wildlife, I see none. At rare spots, though, human life: I see lone shacks burrowed into the Fort Knox of green. I see children playing riverside beside a sign saying *"Kichwa Comunidad"*. I see a couple of clearings with clusters of huts on legs with roofs of woven grass: hands piling sacks or washing clothes or soothing babies. So isolated. Surely a struggle for survival. What are they doing with their lives, living in the boonies like lepers?

What are you doing with yours? I imagine their retort to be. *The jungle, the river: this is life. At one with nature is how people lived for millennia. Your cities are cesspits of humanity, are bubbles of synthetic modernity. Bubbles that will pop. And when World War III starts, this is a smart place to be: no one will nuke the Ecuadoran boondocks.*

Fair point, I'd say. But I need wifi.

Half the passengers leave the boat at Panacocha: a row of askew wooden houses, a path rained into a stream, men at work on motors, and muddy, matted hounds. It was on a map I saw at Coca; in these parts this passes as a town. We're reduced to a handful at Tiputini — a town of sorts but no jetty, only a plank of wood from the boat to the bank — where soldiers board to photo the IDs of those that remain.

After Tiputini is Nuevo Rocafuerte, a godforsaken settlement on the far-flung fringe of Ecuador. Buildings abandoned and discoloured by dampness. Weeds seethe through the roads. Almost deserted. The type of place travellers disappear without a trace, that time to time you hear about on the news: "A British traveller, thirty-five-year-old Mark Walters, visiting Nuevo Rocafuerte on the border of Ecuador and Peru, is missing and presumed dead after local police found a blood-stained Chelsea boot on the banks of the Napo River. In other news, Edinburgh Zoo has a new baby panda . . ."

I walk to a one-room concrete structure with smashed windows and an A4 piece of paper taped to the door: "*Migracion*". Inside is bare: a faded map of Ecuador on the chipped orange walls; a desk with some scraps of paper and a monitor — a cable from it to nothing. A man in shorts and t-shirt stamps me out of Ecuador.

There's no regular service to Pantoja on the Peruvian side of the border. I ask around, looking for someone to take me. Three times I'm quoted £35 — a rip-off for a 30-km ride.

Later I hear German coming from a small boat at the bank. I ask where they're headed.

"Pantoja."

But the old couple who own the boat are shrewd. £30 says the woman, hardly a tooth in the grin that flashes from beneath her yellow beanie. I tell her, with two other passengers, it should be less than that. But she won't budge: £30. At less of a con than £35, she knows I'll bite. And I do. I squeeze in among bikes and canisters, coolers and boxes and a stove, and we set off for Peru.

Gramps stands at the back, hand on the motor; he has a tache and a heavy metal hairdo, wears a baseball cap that says "Naval Captain". Granny snoozes on a filthy mattress on the puddled floor. One of the Germans tells me they just spent three days in the jungle.

"With this pair?" I ask.

"We booked a tour in Coca with their son, but on the day he was ill. So he told his parents to take us."

The other German picks a plaster off his ankle to reveal

a nasty gash. "It was worse before," he tells me. "I cut it and it became infected. But they," — he points at the couple — "took me to see a medicine man in the jungle."

"What did he do?"

"He ground tobacco leaves and mixed them with salt, then boiled the mixture in water to make a paste that he burnt onto the cut. Then he spat on my foot. He spat on it a lot."

"Spat?" I ask, thinking I misheard.

"Yes, spat. I think he was drunk."

"Peru," says Gramps, pointing at the riverbank, where a sad flag hangs from a pole. No fireworks, no confetti, but always a thrill. Ten countries ticked off. One left: Brazil.

Further along, to the left on a hill, camo-painted buildings, a crooked fence, barbed wire, a sign: "*Zona Militar. BSva TACNA N° 27.*" Beside the hill is Pantoja. As we slow to pull up by canoes moored in a fringe of reeds and lily pads, the roar of an engine from behind: a speedboat of sour-faced soldiers racing after us. Gramps is roasted for fifteen minutes by barking, surly men. A pair of pensioners are hardly a threat to national security. They're not even staying in Peru, but returning right away to Nuevo Rocafuerte.

"What's up with him?" I ask one of the Germans, referring to an agitated Gramps.

"There might be a problem with his licence: it's out of date."

"By how long?"

"A year."

A humid village carved into the jungle, Pantoja is as poor as Nuevo Rocafuerte but not a tenth as bleak. No roads. One restaurant. Three gaunt shops. An out-of-order payphone. Some brick buildings and a few concrete, but most are crude-cut wooden bungalows with glassless windows. Hammers pound over the tinny blare of radios. Smoke spirals from skillets that sizzle over coals. Piglets suckle beside scraggly chickens. A lad up a tree picks grapefruit.

I walk up the hill to the immigration office beside the army base that up close resembles a down-at-heel holiday resort. No soldiers at the entrance, only an out-of-proportion silhouette cut-out: the head of a baby on linebacker shoulders with legs like rakes. A sign states: "Join the jungle battalion TACNA N° 27. For the best future for you and your family." A photo below shows men in balaclavas clutching assault rifles. The office is ramshackle but the White House compared to the one at Nuevo Rocafuerte. The gatekeeper — ruby-red lipstick, arms thicker than my neck — stamps me into Peru. I ask her about a boat to Iquitos.

"There's a cheap one for £25."

"When does it leave?"

"Two days ago."

"The next one?"

"Twelve days from now."

"Any other boats?"

"A fast one leaves on Friday. That's £55."

I don't have enough money for the fast boat and a room — if there even is one — for four days. I ask, "Is there an ATM here?"

"No."

PANTOJA TO IQUITOS

To travel is to be blindly optimistic: *I'm sure a boat will come.*
They'll let me aboard, probably. Everything will definitely maybe
be fine. And it was: A boat came the next day. It came from
Iquitos, delivering supplies to villages as part of a government programme, and will return to Iquitos, goods being
picked up and dropped off along the way. Ze Germans and I
struck a deal with the captain: £25 to Iquitos.

A barge coloured curdled-blood and rusty-white, the
Tito II is at least fifty years old. The roof is scattered with
jumble that should be in the trash; weedy plants sprout
from rusted barrels and from a white cross flaps a frayed,
faded Peru flag — the red now pink. The upper deck is
open-sided and open-plan: kitchen and dining table at one
end and TV and chairs at the other; in the middle a couple
of air-mattresses, amid trays of eggs and clumps of bananas
and crates of empty bottles. Half a dozen hammocks — one
of which I'll sleep in — strung across rafters from which
nails poke and the straps of stained, ripped orange life

jackets dangle. Drying shirts drip onto an uneven soldered patchwork that vibrates with the thrum of the engine — in the hold, the size of a Mini, the noise of a tractor. Hammocks in the hold too, where most of the crew sleep. It could be a third-world prison cell: dark, grungy, barred. The sole space of privacy is the cave-like toilet — not a spot to dwell: cramped and a metre from the engine, home to moths and cockroaches. The bridge overlooks a flat-deck loading area that's the width of the boat and a third of its length. Within are a wheel and two levers: fast-slow and ahead-astern. No GPS. The shacks, the bends, the trees: this river to them is as signposted as the Pan-American Highway.

The middle-aged captain does most of his captaining from a hammock. He scratches his moustache and caresses a paunch that bulges through a white vest. His little black eyes watch cheesy dramas on an old TV. His wife is the cook; their two kids live on board. The crew take turns at the wheel; there are eight of them, short but sturdy blokes in their twenties and thirties. None speak English. One wears Bayern Munich football shorts. "*Munchen*," says a grinning German to the guy, pointing at the shorts then himself.

"*Eh?*" is the reply.

"*Munchen. Alemania*," tries the German.

"*Munchen es en Espana,*" says the guy.

"*No,*" insists the German. "*Munchen es en Alemania.*"

"*No. Espana.*"

The guy is positive that Munich is in Spain and won't be persuaded otherwise, even by a German who lives in Munich. To be fair, until recently, I didn't know where Caracas or Quito were. And, I suspect, many on the streets of Munich and Manchester wouldn't be able to name the capital of Paraguay or Bolivia or Peru.

Another worker asks to borrow my earphones. I'd let him keep them but worry about getting replacements. It's simple to purchase earphones *on* Amazon, less so *in* the Amazon.

The first stop is at a primitive village of rustic huts. We nudge into the bank and guys leap down and chuck on board yuca and bananas and grapefruits. Freaking chickens with bound feet are placed inside a tyre on the roof. Tied to a post near the bank is a bull that's front foot is limp and raw. It's to come on board and a tug-of-war ensues. A second bull readies for a charge to help his pal, but flees when stones are thrown. The first rallies for an escape, pulling over two men as it runs off. More hands seize the rope and in the bull is reeled. It still resists — and its mate returns for a second rescue; again aborted when it's attacked — but with that maimed front foot it has no hope. Have they wounded it on purpose, I wonder, to make it weak? A disabled animal fights less. Minutes later it's trussed in a harness by the side of the boat. It sways as it's heaved upwards on a chain, several sets of hands at work. Its eyes bulge and its dong flops; slops of shit slide out its ass. Once aboard its horns are tied low to a pole and its tail is snapped. It slumps, still but for a shiver. A bucket of water to wash away the shit. Water, though, can't wash away the sin. I only watched the shameful spectacle, but I'm still guilty. A meat-eater, I'm part of the demand. I'll become vegetarian, starting right now.

A trail of light waves in our wake as we ride on along the Napo past marshes and swamps and lagoons. It bubbles, ripples, swirls; is dirty brown, too cloudy to see below the surface. It spreads to a couple of kilometres. It shrinks to a few hundred metres. Sometimes it splinters into three or four then converges downriver. At times it's almost placid — and that with its size makes it look more of a lake than a river. Moss-covered trunks float by like embryonic islands and wooden canoes glide along the margins. Left, right, left, right go the small paddles; the paddlers as often children as they are adults. A panorama of the Amazon slides past: vast, dense, untamed wilderness. Snatches of scenes within the green, remoteness penetrated for a second: I see tatty shacks on stilts, some of which have only two walls (or if you're a glass-half-full person: two very large windows). I see hands scoop water over heads as people crouch riverside showering. I see a naked little lad — with one hand he waves, with one he hides his willy. The sporadic settlements have a church and a school, some a soccer pitch — crooked branches for goalposts. I've not seen a hospital. Tobacco and phlegm might cure a minor infection, but chlamydia or cancer? Coca is more than a day away, as is Iquitos — and that's in a motorboat; in a canoe, a week or more. The dark, small people descend from the Incas and life is little different for them than it was for their ancestors. Cocooned from progress, it's as if half a millennium hasn't happened. What I see is much the same as that seen by the eyes of the conquistadors. On a posh boat — with a bed, no bulls: that type of boat — a ride like this through a National Geographic landscape would sell for thousands.

Lunch is served: yellowy, watery, beefy soup. Rude to say no. I panic after I eat it: *Was that Bullseye?* I check if he's still whole. He is. And he's on his feet. He wasn't sedated, only defeated. I pat his hind: "Don't worry, buddy; you're going on a little holiday to where the grass is greener and there are seventy-two virgin cows."

His head turns wearily. "Are there people there?" his dull eyes seem to ask.

"No."

"Good. They're bastards."

"We are, yeah. Sorry."

"This magic place I'm going, what's it called?"

"Tesco."

I again pledge to become vegetarian. It's the most time I've spent with a bovine, and I'm certain he's sentient. A being ended — one with a friend; his pal this morning, remember, trying to save him — to sate a belly for a few hours. It's not right. And if not for Bullseye and his bros, for the Amazon. A fifth of it has gone and cattle ranching accounts for over half the loss — other causes are plantations and logging and mining. If deforestation continues at the current rate, by 2030 a quarter of it will be treeless. And as the Amazon suffers, so does the world: deforestation constitutes 10% of global greenhouse gas emissions.

We make more stops. One at a shack propped mid-river, a sort of river service station. On its porch are a cat, two dogs, several children; people out front in canoes natter and drink from bowls. On come five sacks, armfuls of yuca, two tortoises, and a duck. Off goes a box of chocolate in a motor dinghy; it returns without the chocolate but with a man. Doesn't seem fair: a man is worth at least three boxes of chocolate. This bloke, though, is broken — suffered a stroke, I think — so maybe one box is fair. He can't climb the steps to the upper deck so is put in the hold with the duck and the tortoises.

Further on, a clearing on the bank. No one's there. "Johnny," someone shouts from the boat.

Nothing.

"Johnny," he calls again.

Nothing.

Hands to his mouth to amplify: "Johnny."

Nothing.

"Johnny, Johnny, Johnny," he tries, adding repetition to amplification.

Nothing.

"JOHNNY," shout three guys.

Nothing.

"JOHNNY!" everyone shouts.

It must be important, whatever they want him for.

A woman appears. She asks, "Who do you want?"

"Johnny."

"He's not here."

"Give him these bread rolls."

Dinner is noodles and chicken — one from the roof; I saw it taken into the kitchen. After I eat it — I really don't like to be rude — for the third time today I resolve to become vegetarian. Bullseye, for his meal, is tossed bananas. He eats them whole, peel and all. Sentient but stupid.

Cows on the bank at a later drop-off. "Where are you going?" moos one.

"Tesco," replies Bullseye.

"Lucky you. My sister went last year. She liked it so much she's yet to come back."

Bullseye smiles.

The sausage munchers — big-footed, wooden Tobias and campish Cristoff — are cycling from Colombia to Chile. They work on their bikes to mend the wear and tear from the four days it took them to cycle to Coca.

"How much was that?" asks the captain, pointing at Tobias's badass bike.

"$1000."

I'd have lied. If we smash into something and start to sink, the captain will rescue a $1000 bike before three worthless foreigners.

Then the krauts erect their tent. "Leafcutter ants in the jungle," explains Cristoff, referring to the dozens of holes. They take photos of the holes before taping them up, hoping to claim on insurance: "Hallo, I vould zlike to make ze claimien. I vas in ze junglestein, and ze ants, ze scheissers, munchen mein tenthausen." I doubt that will be believed: Ants ate my tent is as lame as the dog ate my homework.

A veil of black settles. The jungle merges with the night sky. The dark water reflects a corridor of moonlight. Lightning flashes. Soon after, a light blinks on the bank. The boat slows, edges to the side. A man shouts that he has goods to sell. A torch scans the bank for a safe spot to stop. Tiny faces briefly illuminated, eyes shining brightly: the man's many kids. Goods are loaded: pineapples, sugar cane, bananas, yuca. The jungle and the dark add a sense of illegality like it's contraband rather than fruit and veg. As we pull away the front of the boat rips at a cord that stretches to the man's hut. It looks like the hut will fall. It leans. It groans. Then the cord snaps. The man rages, but we ride on.

At the next stop, no goods and no man. *"Peru. Escocia,"* says one of the workers, excitedly. They crowd the TV on stools and chairs. It's football: Peru v Scotland. We've stopped because we've picked up a signal. The buildup shows the streets of Lima packed with wild fans: flags and scarves, singing and dancing and drinking. The country has World Cup fever. This game is only a friendly in preparation, but I understand the enthusiasm: Peru last qualified for a World Cup in 1982. My grandfather is Scottish, which makes me a quarter tartan. I hate haggis and think Andy Murray is a wanker, so more like 23%. But I'll cheer on Peru so I don't have to swim to Iquitos. On the tiny TV the ball is the size of a crumb and the players look like ants. Peru win 2-0.

I struggle to sleep after the match: the engine drones and a bulb burns bright and Tobias's stinking size-16s swing an inch from my nose. It could, though, be worse: I could be Señor Stroke in the hold beside a shitting Bullseye.

IQUITOS

Iquitos reminds me of Vietnam, Thailand, Cambodia. The traffic and tuk-tuks and stray dogs, the street stalls and grotty food-halls and down-and-dirty hotels. A taste of Asia that I miss. But I'm not here for the city. I'm here for ayahuasca, the hardcore hallucinogen that's stronger than LSD. William S. Burroughs — the original ayahuasca tourist in the 1950s — said it was the strongest substance he'd ever experienced. "It is like nothing else," he said. "This is not the chemical lift of C, the sexless, horribly sane stasis of junk, the vegetable nightmare of peyote, or the humorous silliness of weed . . . This is insane overwhelming rape of the senses . . . It is space-time travel . . . You make migrations, incredible journeys . . ."

"Meet outside Restaurante Fitzcarraldo at 11am," said the email. A guy comes for us — a Swiss girl and me. He's a tall, wiry yank in his forties with beaming blue-grey eyes. His head is shaved; his greying beard is a few inches long, an embryonic Gandalf. His t-shirt says "Keep On Floatin'". We ride a tuk-tuk to Puerto Bellavista-Nanay in the outskirts. At the port is what looks like a voodoo market. A croc head fried, its teeth still intact. Juicy larvae skewered through sticks; others writhing, dozens per bowl. We squash into a long-tail boat with locals. Greg says it will take an hour. "We're the last stop."

As we skim along the churning brown river — the actual Amazon — I ask Greg how he ended up working at an ayahuasca centre in Peru. He says he visited as a guest a year ago and had a life-changing experience. "Ayahuasca said to me that to become a shaman is my path. It felt like a future self had reached back to me in the present. When I went back to the States I quit my job in IT."

"You told them why?"

"I told them I was moving to Peru to become a shaman."

"Any raised eyebrows?"

"Yeah."

I ask how long it takes to become a shaman.

"Four to ten years."

He's been in Peru for five months. I ask if he's done any shamanism so far.

He says, "Sometimes they let me sit on a chair up front and shake my chakapa."

"Your what?" I say, wondering if that's a euphemism.

"Chakapa; it's a leaf rattle."

He starts to play a fantasy game on his phone. I start to wonder if I've made a terrible mistake.

We get off the boat at the largely wooden village of Santa Maria; from there a half-hour trudge into the damp, humid jungle to La Luna del Amazonas. We come to a clearing, a scout-hut-like building with green mesh walls. Water drips into pots from the leaky frond roof. A long table and brown sofas and shelves of books: *The Psychedelic Explorer's Guide*; *The Tibetan Book of the Dead*; *DMT: The Spirit Molecule*; *The Doors of Perception*; *Zen is Eternal Life*. Trippy paintings: an anaconda on an orange river, a naked goddess zapping energy at a figure suspended within an orb. A stuffed jaguar paw and a pack of green powder labelled *Anti-Inflammatory Vaginal Powder*. "That's peyote, actually," Greg says. "It's sold at the market in Iquitos. They label it wrongly for tourists that want to take it home." And four sacks of what appear to be chopped branches. Greg says its a vine called banisteriopsis caapi, one of the two ingredients of ayahuasca. The other is a shrub named psychotria viridis, which contains dimethyltryptamine (DMT), a potent psychedelic. It's brewed onsite, the vines and shrub boiled together for twelve hours to create a viscous brown liquid. On shelves I see some: half a dozen plastic bottles filled with the muddy potion.

With Greg are two other "facilitators": American Gia and Brit Shati. They're huggers not hand-shakers. Gia, like Greg, came to the centre as a guest before returning to volunteer — they get free food and board and ayahuasca as payment. Gia takes Swiss Girl and me on a tour of the grounds. Spread around, and each separate from the others, are a dozen shacks for guests. Mesh walls absorb the ambience of the rainforest. A bed, desk, and chair inside. No power. No locks. Next Gia takes us to the "temple", where tonight we'll drink ayahuasca in a "ceremony". It's an octagonal structure that resembles an upturned wicker bowl. It has mesh walls and a dirt floor cracked like crazy paving. Five chairs and a low table lined at the front, behind which are dreamcatchers and a painting of a jungle scene. Seven mattresses on either side, a few inches apart; on each a pillow and a blanket, a bog roll and a bowl — because ayahuasca causes people to "purge" (aka vomit), which is said to purify the body. Gia says, "We don't talk during or after the ceremony; not until the following morning. And we ask you not to leave during the ceremony."

On the way out, right outside the temple, I jump and shriek: "A tarantula!"

Gia looks at it: "Don't worry. It's dead."

Swiss Girl and I aren't the only guests; there are a few others, each in search of something — a cure or direction or spirituality, a journey to the hinterland of subconsciousness — and their search has brought them to the Amazon, to ayahuasca. We sit around, chatting. I say that I read that some people swear they met God when drinking ayahuasca, and ask Greg if he's met anyone who's said that.

"A few, yeah; more say Jesus. Even Shati, who's Hindu, said she's seen Jesus."

"Elves and pixies?" I ask. "Little green men?"

"Yeah, some have," he says. "Ayahuasca shows people what they need to see and tells them what they need to know in ways that they'll remember."

"Sounds like fun," I say.

"It can be," he says. "But if it is, that's a bonus."

Someone talks about visits to other realms. One says, "Yesterday ayahuasca showed me that I was once a Roman. I relived that whole lifetime last night." She says we've all lived before, hundreds of times. Another person has misplaced their passport and plans to ask "Mother Ayahuasca" where it is and is sure that she'll know — and is assured by someone else that she will. But much of the talk is the typical mundane: moaning about a toothache; how much toilet paper to buy on the next visit to Iquitos.

Most guests, I'm told, visit for a fortnight and consume ayahuasca four times per week. A few stay for months, like a Swede who's just left after being here for ten weeks. Greg tells me, "When that guy came he was broken, barely alive; monosyllabic, ate almost nothing, hung out by himself. As he drank ayahuasca he felt himself opening, feeling things he hadn't felt for many years. When he left he was reanimated, like brand new."

That gives hope to a Londoner woman who's been here a week and sees ayahuasca as last-chance saloon: "I've done everything: all the kinds of therapy there are on the NHS; other therapies that I paid a lot for; five kinds of anti-depressants."

Snake oil, some will say, pseudo-spiritual nonsense: psychedelics are party drugs not medicines. But recent scientific research has confirmed the potential of hallucinogens to alleviate depression, addictions, traumas. A rebrand is required to convince the masses. If DMT and psilocybin came as pills and were branded with a snappy sci-fi-like moniker — as Prozac, Zoloft, and Paxil have — people wouldn't think twice. Though it occurs naturally in the human body — and has been linked to dreams and near-death-experiences — DMT remains illegal practically everywhere. Class A in the UK. Schedule 1 in the US. In these parts, though — Peru, Ecuador, Colombia — it's 100% legal. Used for centuries and seen as a sort of sacrament. In Quechua, the local language, the word *ayahuasca* translates to "vine of the soul". Others translate it to "vine of death".

Ayahuasca can't solve problems, Greg says, but it can suggest solutions. Or show that it's not a problem that matters and thus can be let go.

Gia says, "It shows you the path to take. You then need to do the work."

Ayahuasca aids reflection, I'm told; it can let you see what you've been blind to. Greg says, "It's like a mirror. A brutal mirror sometimes. You might not like what you see."

It's spoken about with reverence. No one talks of getting high nor alludes to tonight's ceremony being a party. The whole set-up is serious, not least the strict dietary regime: Two meals a day — 9am and 1pm — and no snacking outside those times. No salt or sugar, meat or dairy, caffeine or alcohol — all on the no-no list for a week before coming (as well as no sex).

And there's paperwork: a consent form I sign says: "Effects produced by ayahuasca may include changes in your perception of reality . . . access to detailed memories that you thought you'd forgotten . . . paranormal phenomena . . . and perinatal or transpersonal experiences (in which you may experience your own death and rebirth.) You may experience nausea, vomiting, chills, dizziness, diarrhoea, tremors, sweating, and ataxia . . . panic attacks or psychotic episodes . . . depersonalisation, psychosis, or delirium."

I also have to complete a medical questionnaire; it asks about any history of psychiatric disorders. I might be mental, but as it hasn't been officially diagnosed, I tick no to everything.

Gia tried DMT on herself before she came here. She vaped the substance — which results in a supercharged fifteen-minute experience, compared to the several hours that ayahuasca lasts for. Her solo trial didn't go well: "Afterwards I had a feeling of a presence on my back, something that had attached itself to me when DMT took me to other worlds. I had to go to Miami to visit a shaman to help me; as soon as I walked into the room he saw it straight away: an evil being on my back. He spent forty minutes scraping the thing off me."

Which is why, she says — and Greg agrees — that shamans are essential to the ayahuasca experience: to combat malign spirits.

They have a few shamans at La Luna del Amazonas, Greg says, but it's Benigno who will conduct tonight's ceremony. He's eighty-something, one of the oldest shamans in Iquitos. Greg says Benigno first drank ayahuasca when he was six.

That, I say, seems way too young.

He says, "We give kids vaccines at that age, and here they look at it in the same way: if they don't give them ayahuasca, then they're not protected."

Benigno was born in Santa Maria, and this centre is an extension of the village clinic where he helps people "suffering from witchcraft" and diagnoses illnesses. "Ayahuasca lets a shaman see the source of the issue," Greg says. "Then they use other plants to heal." Which is why locals call them healers (*curanderos*). Also *maestros*, meaning teachers.

I say, "Is there a *proper* doctor in Santa Maria? With a stethoscope and needles?"

"No," says Greg. "Only the shaman."

I ask if Benigno (who only comes for the ceremony) will

wear a grass skirt and a headdress — like, you know, in the movies.

He says, "There are shamans that do, more so in the Shipibo tradition. Ours wear jeans and shirts."

At 8pm we file along a dirt path to the temple. We each settle on a mattress. With our pyjama-like clothing, it could almost be a sleepover. But the mood is eerie and solemn, spooky as a seance. Four half-melted candles in the centre, arranged as a diamond; their flicker the only light. The rain-forest around is a panorama of Rorschach images, a sound-track of obscure noises. At the front, shrouded in shadow, are two seated figures talking in hushed tones. On the table is a bottle opaque with the occult elixir; over it Benigno murmurs incantations in Quechua and Spanish. He tokes a roll-up and blows smoke at the bottle. He flicks his fingers at the air on all sides — as if shooing something — and makes wind-like sounds: *swoosh*, *whoosh*. His shaky hands decant a half-inch measure into a cup. He holds it to his face and whispers at it. He passes it to his apprentice, who takes it to the woman on the nearest mattress. She holds it in front of her, reflects silently for a second, then says "*Salud Maestro*" and drinks. My turn next. It tastes like burnt tyres. The process repeats for each person — except for Greg, tonight's non-drinker, on hand to assist anyone freaking. After Benigno and his sidekick drink, the candles are blown out.

Darkness. Stillness. Silence.

For half an hour, nothing happens. Then a slow dance of sound: a cross between muffled maracas and shoes being wiped on a mat: *che-che-che-che-che-che-che-che-che-che-che-che-che*. Benigno starts to sing *icaros*: sacred chants, lullaby-like melodies, Spanish mixed with Quechua. The only words I understand: "*ayahuasca*" and "*naturales*" and "*plantas*" and "*limpiar*". At times he whistles rather than sings. I sense shifting and shuffling around the room but see only shadow and silhouette. I feel normal, wonder what the fuss is about. Then reality unravels ...

"... *de de de la la li* ... *da da li la la la* ... *de de de la la li* ... *da da li la la la* ..." *Che-che-che-che-che-che-che-che-che-che-che-che-che.* *Bleeegh. Cough. Blargh.* Yawning. So much yawning. A faint, breathy whistle. Hocking, spitting. *Blargh.* A ghostly greenish luminescence. Bruised clouds close in. *Aah ooh*, rustles and murmurs, *bleh, bleh, bleh. Che-che-che-che-che-che-che-che-che-che-che-che-che.* Waves of vertigo. Boiling. Blistering. On my stomach; grasping my pillow. Turned inside out. Tormented. *Cough, cough, cough. Blargh. Che-che-che-che-che-che-che-che-che-che-che-che-che.* *Bleeegh.* Lowered into a hole: down, down, down, down into the dark, damp earth. Faces crying: friends, family. Spade by spade I'm buried. *Che-che-che-che-che-che-che-che-che-che-che-che-che.* Colourless and cramped, echoes and drips. Atmosphere nocturnal, miasmic. Fungi and spores; spiders, beetles, slugs. Dementors prodding, tongues stuck out, eyes venomous. "... *de de de la la li* ... *da da li la la la* ..." Can't spew, can't stand, can't speak. Delusions within delusions within delusions. Fragmented, cascading thoughts. That fucking sorcerer: bedevilled by his black arts. That hell-broth, coursing insidiously through my bloodstream. Need to get it out. *Cough. Blargh. Bleeegh.* Shapeshifting slobbering creatures; odious, oozing tentacles; clawing and pawing. Chorus of misery, guttural and grotesque: *Wuh-uh-uh-uh.* *Braaah. Uh-oh. Ugh.* Elephant with the face of a fly: "Look at this that you did. People don't forget." *Che-che-che-che-che-che-che-che-che-che-che-che-che-che.* Wobble. Lumber. Collapse. Try to crawl to an escape, but reeled in, returned. "Dawn, come dawn, fade out the dark." The flick of a lighter, a flash of a face set solid: a hideous gargoyle. ". . . *de de de la la li . . . da da li la la la . . . de de de la la li . . . da da li la la li . . .*" Stop, I beg you. STOP. "You bought a ticket for the ride; the ride you're taking." *Che-che-che-che-che-che-che.* *Blargh.* *Che-che-che-che-che-che-che.* *Cough, cough.* Swampy, filthy place: again and again. Horrific, darkening. *Drip drop drip drop drop drop drop.* Dead matter flowing. *Argh.* Head is a ghost train. *Aya, aya, aya.* *Hmpf.* Mouth is quicksand. Retching horrors and weeds. Sobbing somewhere. *Bleeegh.* Squirming larvae. *Blargh.* Freezing. *Che-che-che-che-che-che-che.* Alive? Or not? Here how many years? A voice — who? — says, "This is reality; all else is illusion." *Che-che-che-che-che-che-che-che-che-che-che-che-che.* "Come on, son, come on." Tar-like surface: can't break through. "Come on, Mark." Tears. Hands out. Too far apart to touch. "Mark . . ." Gurgle, gasp. Sinking: so heavy. Dooooooown. "Meester, your melan-chocolate!" My what? *Waaaaaaa.* Opium den, man? Looks it. *Cough, cough.* Police there? Ha, no. *Hissssssss.* You out. And you: Damn snakes! *Tsk,* ta-ta, *grrrrrr.* Hear me? Wallowing in squelchy sludge. Limping after me, my brain. Mind's a madman's, a cancerous carousel. Drunk what? Poison? *Wallala leialala.* Birdman uttering and rapping. Fingers stroking. *Schweep-schwoop, shoo-shoo-shoo.* Last rites? *Da-die-da-die-deeeee.* Eyes gone: no clue. BANG. Again alone, adrift; nearly suffocating in this cesspool. *Pop-pop, shlick.* Grappling reptiles — so slimy. Cunt Jesus coming? Come now. NOW. Thousands of me? I is me? *Whooooooffff, prrrrrrrvt. Kata-kata.*

Krrrrrrr. 999. "Hello?" Es Señor Schizofreud. So severed. Fragile: been far — too far. Fuck, fuck, yes, fuck. "*. . . limpiar . . . limpiar . . . limpiar . . .*" Stone. Hand. Roll. Between thumb and finger: rolling. *Cough. Blargh. Che-che-che-che-che-che-che-che-che-che-che-che-che.* Think. Focus. Names, faces: pull out? "*. . . de de de la la li . . . ayahuasca . . .*" Thinking, rolling. Temple? *Cough, cough, cough. Che-che-che-che-che-che-che-che-che-che-che-che-che.* Roll, roll, roll. See the temple for a second. Then back in that inky, toxic abyss. "You're alone. You're mine," says a hooded reaper figure. "*. . . plantas . . . naturales . . . de de de la la li . . . da da li la la la. . .*" This shadowy noxious swamp, I think, as I roll, is those listless days where I loathe the world, retreat to my room, talk to no one. Days that add up to weeks and months. *Bleeegh.* "*. . . de de de la la li . . . da da li la la la . . . ayahuasca . . . ayahuasca . . . ayahuasca . . . de de de la la li . . . da da li la la la . . .*" Roll and think, think and roll. Family and friends: when I'm with them, I'm not here. I think of times with them. A calm comes. The void fades. "*. . . ayahuasca . . . ayahuasca . . . ayahuasca . . .*" I roll the stone, roll, roll, roll, and think of what I left, think how they miss me when I'm gone. Roll and think of seven months of nothing familiar, no one to call a friend. Family unable to pull me out meant something: me here in the Amazon; them there, out of reach. I roll and roll and think and think of those I love, who love me. I've long been distant, a stranger to those I know; this journey and others, travelling a decade. Tomorrow I'll return to the familiar, to friends and family. I've come far to find home.

EPILOGUE

That ending was bizarre, unexpected; I should explain...

I was tripping my balls off, that's for sure. Utter nonsense? Or did it mean something? What to make of all that, I'm still not sure now.

But even after dawn at last came, I had a clear feeling that I had to go home. The seed had been planted. Or, perhaps, the seed was there already and blossomed through ayahuasca. Perhaps Ayahuasca visualised my subconscious, made me see how I felt.

I say the seed may have been there already because I'd been down, was out of juice. It's not all ice creams and beaches; a marathon, more like. And a marathon is tough — so they say, and I'm prepared to take their word for it so I don't have to run one. Travel at times is sweat, tears, pain; it's testing, draining, despite the many larks on the way. It's worth it at the end, when you look back and think, *Wow; look what I did*. But in the midst of it, it can be: *Why the fuck am I doing this?*

Things get a little messy as the miles go on. I start to fray — don't sleep or eat as well as I need to. Then there were the drugs: A cause of decline? Or a symptom? Either way, they were yet more of a drain. It doesn't take all that much to knock me out of sync (and I'm not that robust to start with); when that happens, darkness and doubt to deal with. Some days on this trip I'd barely leave my room. I could be out of action for up to a week. I started in Los Angeles at 100%. At times after, I was down to fumes.

So I flew home — Iquitos to Lima to Miami to London to Birmingham — and a week after being a wreck in the Amazon (*Che-che-che-che-che-che-che. Blargh. Cough, cough . . .*), I was sat in a hot bath, sipping a Nespresso, nibbling Marks & Spencer's biscuits.

Bliss.

In Birmingham I stayed to write this book. And there I stayed for my first British Christmas for seven years. I pulled the crackers ("What do you call a deer with no eyes?") and I ate the turkey (Sorry, Bullseye) and I got new boxers (thanks Mum).

It was good. The right choice.

I'll be sure to be in the UK more; to be more of a son, more of a brother, a better friend.

I don't regret stopping the journey when I did. Los Angeles to the Amazon is a damn long way, and I saw a lot, and much did I learn. I didn't quite make it to Brazil, to Rio de Janeiro; the next country — so close, yet SO far: Rio is 4,000 km from Iquitos. But Los Angeles, Rio de Janeiro: those are just two names on a map; it's in between where lay the stories . . .

The high wall, barbed wire, spotlights, cameras, patrol

cars, guards: MEXICO. The ride with the *chicas* down the hole-studded highway through the Valle de los Cirios, cacti casting strange shadows on the scalded terrain. Convoys of pickup trucks with swivel-mounted weaponry; sullen soldiers at checkpoints — "They're looking for guns, drugs, things like that." The ferry across the tranquil, turquoise Gulf of California to Topolobampo. From *Pueblo Magico* El Fuerte, the Ferrocarril Chihuahua al Pacifico through Narcoland, slithering through the Sierra Madre Occidental. Zip-lining across the vertigo-inducing *Barrancas del Cobre* — "Na, na, na, na, na, na, na, na, na, na, na, na, Batmaaaaaan!" The battered minivan to neat and sweet, narco-run Batoplias, with its thuggish hombres and its abandoned silver mine. At Palenque in Mexico's jungled humid south, the Mayan metropolis once ruled by a twelve-year-old martian. Snakes, scorpions, Americans. "I did not have sexual relations with that monkey." The border at El Ceibo: a man the size of two men, biceps as thick as my neck — *"No pagas, no te vas."* The locals' *colectivos* to Sayaxche to Coban — socks stuffed with money, speakers blasting eighties synth-pop — through the densely-forested mountainscape of Alta Verapaz; then the psychedelic-painted "chicken bus" from Salama to scummy Guatemala City. The shite Hotel Reforma, a film set for a suicide. The Frodo-like ascent of Acatenango in a ladies coat. Fuego, the Devil's chimney, violently hiccuping — "Motherfucker beautiful." Birding barefoot in the Cerro Azul Meambar National Park: the Red-legged Honeycreeper, the Violet Sabrewing, the Gartered Trogon. Beside Lake Yojoa, the shed pub — pints of Porter Cafetero, of Pena Blanca. Ernesto and his thirty-two brothers. In gritty, greyified Tegucigalpa, the failed *revolucion*: gas and stones traded in scrappy skirmishes — "GL-203/T. TRIPLE TEAR GAS CHARGE. Do not use after expiration date." The drawer of cocaine at the Iguanas Hostal. The Mad Hatters: Horse Face and Gerbil Chops. Fleeing to Matagalpa on a beat-up yellow school bus. The pitiful places, befouled and trash-strewn, en route to the mud pit El Rama. John and his chats with whales, his madcap conspiracies. The *panga* along the murky Rio Escondido to fishy, faded Bluefields. The spewy voyage to rugged paradise Little Corn Island: its palmy beaches and reggaeton and spiced English — "Ju wan some ganja, mon?" Cows that swim and hellish crocodiles in the Rio San Juan; sweatily squelching through the barbarous landscape of the Indio Maiz Biological Reserve, the stomping ground of pumas and man-eating boars — "They left nothing of him. No bones, not even his hair." At Refugio de Vida Silvestre Laguna Urpiano: The Markimum Extreme Sand Shoveller v8; an extra hundred thousand turtles in the sea — Michelangelo, Donatello, Kermit . . . In rough-edged Puerto Viejo: Rasta Ralcetin and his jerk chicken pan, Mike the bomb-making terrorist — "I was gonna blow up some shit." And a lucky escape with Cornrows and the cops. Sweaty, slurping cruise-shippers shuffling around Casco Viejo; tumbledown Caledonia and El Chorrillo. The manmade miracle that's the canal. Viking Thor, the free citizen — "Western political bastards. Fuckers, all of them." The Big Fish II — "It won the Admiral's Cup." — with lollipop-sucking Francia — "Darling, don't leave it on; the boat will explode." — and Aussie Sam: "Why's that bloke brought a surfboard into the jungle?" Sand so fine, so white and sugar-like, at the San Blas Islands, where live the midget Gunas —

part gypsy, part Oompa Loompa. Forty-eight hours non-stop sailing across open sea to the north coast of Colombia, the twinkling orange lights of the colonial treasure Cartagena; its city walls and fountains and courtyards, its colourful mansions with flowering balconies. "White coffee" — *snnii-iffff*. On the slopes of the Aburra Valley, the labyrinthine, favela-style barrios of Medellin. The hill of trash, Voldemort's football pitch. "If he killed your child, your sibling, your parent: how many houses would he need to build to make up for it?" The road out of sleepy, quaint Jardin — wildly wooded, torrenting waterfalls, rockfaces collapsing — on a broken bus driven by a double denim believer. Eje Cafetero, the coffee-growing Andean foothills; the crawl up switchbacks slicked by showers. Peaks and gorges, green and mist. The eel-like descent into the Quindio Pass, through Cajamarca, through Cocora, through Ibague. Checkpoints in Cauca: sandbag bunkers; vehicles topped with heavy guns. The Andes again, on a road scratched on the mountainside; all but a metre ahead veiled white — the ravines, the peaks, the road: gone. At Ipiales, a couple of Fishermen and a thousand Venezuelan refugees — "The currency is so worthless that you could wallpaper a building with bills for less than the cost of paint." The ride east across Ecuador to Coca: inside the bus, The Rock running along a beach in Speedos; outside it, wet-and-wild woodlands, greenness glistening. At Coca, onto the Transporte Fluvial Kamu Kamu #4; skimming along the fast-flowing mud-brown Rio Napo into the Amazon — 390 billion trees! Godforsaken Nuevo Rocafuerte; onto a boat with "Naval Captain" Gramps and Ze Germans — "Ze ants, ze scheissers, munchen mein tenthausen." — from there to Pantoja, chased by a speedboat of sour-faced soldiers. The Tito II for the next leg of the Napo; pick ups — Señor Stroke — and drop offs — "JOHN-NY!" — along the route through vast, dense, untamed wilderness to a-taste-of-Asia Iquitos. The damp, humid jungle, La Luna del Amazonas, with Beardy Greg — "Keep On Floatin'" — shaking his chakapa and eighty-something Benigno singing icaros — "... *ayahuasca* ... *de de de la la li* ... *da da li la la la* ..." — as reality unravelled ...

Experiences, memories: banked forever.

As for Brazil, it will still be there — though with less trees — a few years from now. I'll go there, write a book. Also one about Africa. And Japan. And the Mekong. And the Middle East. And ...

WRITE A REVIEW

A rating, a few words: it only takes a minute. And it helps authors like me a lot.

You can write a review on Amazon or Goodreads. A list of links to the review pages on those websites are listed at www.marktries.com/amerzonia/review (Note: You can write a review on Amazon even if you didn't buy the book from Amazon.)

Thanks

Mark

mark@marktries.com

www.marktries.com

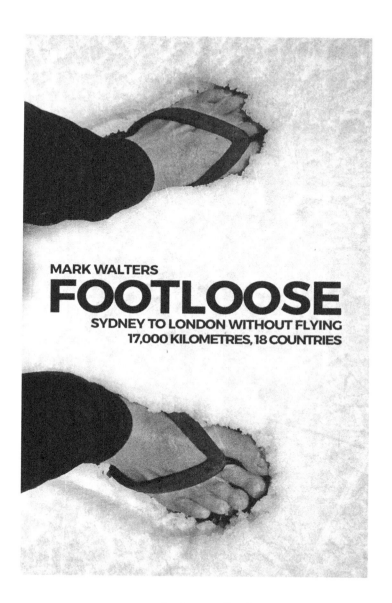

MARK WALTERS

FOOTLOOSE
SYDNEY TO LONDON WITHOUT FLYING
17,000 KILOMETRES, 18 COUNTRIES

www.marktries.com/footloose

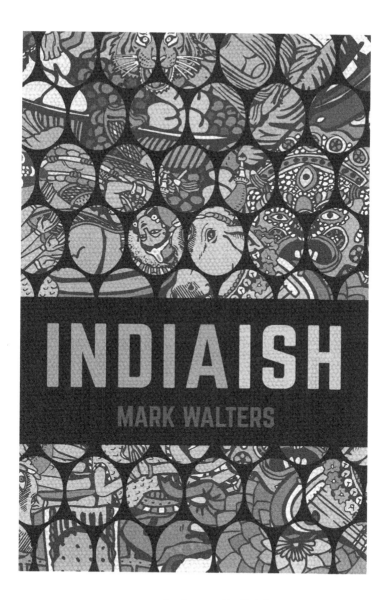

INDIAISH

MARK WALTERS

www.marktries.com/indiaish

Made in the USA
Monee, IL
01 November 2020

46541542R00135